PAUL BARRUEL

BIRDS OF THE WORLD

Their Life and Habits

WITH 310 PHOTOGRAPHS AND DRAWINGS
INCLUDING 94 IN COLOUR

Prefaced by
PROFESSOR FRANÇOIS BOURLIÈRE

Translated by
PHYLLIS BARCLAY-SMITH
with additional material by
CHARLES JOHNSON

NEW EDITION
ENTIRELY RESET

New York
OXFORD UNIVERSITY PRESS
1973

CONTENTS

First published in Great Britain 1954
by GEORGE G. HARRAP & CO. LTD
182–184 High Holborn, London WC1V 7AX

New edition entirely reset 1973

© George G. Harrap & Co. Ltd 1954, 1973

Library of Congress Catalogue Card Number 73-76912

Typeset in Great Britain by Western Printing Services Ltd, Bristol
PRINTED IN FRANCE

PREFACE

*W*hen inaugurating a new series devoted to the wonders of nature it would be difficult to find a better subject than the life of birds. As a matter of fact birds, with butterflies and fish, are the most popular with a section of the public, which daily becomes more numerous. This is not surprising, as their curious behaviour is generally linked with graceful or strange forms and sometimes vivid colours. The majority are diurnal, carrying on their activities in broad daylight and presenting innumerable problems to anyone interested in nature. With a good pair of field-glasses, a field-guide, patience, method and luck, any intelligent observer is capable of entering into their lives and making his own contribution to ornithology.

In recent years the study of birds has become a real science. An increasing number of observations made by enthusiastic naturalists—simple amateurs or professional scientists—has changed and considerably extended the boundaries of classical ornithology. The list of the various forms inhabiting our globe being more or less complete, the attention of naturalists has gradually turned towards the study of habits (ethology), and of the complex relationship of birds with their habitats (ecology). These last two subjects have made great strides during the last twenty years, and at the present time the study of birds in the field has become as important for the biologist as their study in the laboratory. What previously was merely a pleasant amateur pastime has now become one of the most live branches of modern zoology with contacts in the realms of psychology, physiology, sociology, and evolution.

Few people are better qualified than Paul Barruel to present a general picture of the biology of birds. Artist and naturalist, Paul Barruel knows how to combine scientific precision with charm in description. His erudition is only equalled by his knowledge of birds in the wild, and the reader can be assured that every opinion in this book is based on a multitude of careful observations and precise facts.

It was not the author's intention in these two hundred pages to review all available information, and to support each sentence with numerous references or footnotes. The works quoted in the bibliography will provide the reader with any supplementary information and details he may desire. On the contrary, the aim has been by making "pictures talk" to endeavour to reach as wide a public as possible, sportsmen as well as naturalists. The text of the book simply aims at an outline of the more important facts and at forming a link between them and the photographs. In this respect I should like to thank our colleagues, both in Europe and other continents who have enabled us to publish a beautiful collection of biological pictures. In particular I have to thank my friends, Guy Mountfort, Secretary of the British Ornithologists' Union, and Monsieur Paul Géroudet, Editor-in-Chief of Nos Oiseaux, who respectively introduced us to British and Swiss photographers. I must not omit Mr O. Svanberg, thanks to whom the remarkable photographs of our Swedish colleagues have enriched this volume. To them is undoubtedly owed a great deal of the success of this book.

*

Twenty years have passed since the original publication of Birds of the World by Paul Barruel. Reprinted several times in its original French version and translated into a dozen languages, this book has become one of the classics of ornithology, and a whole generation of enthusiastic amateurs is indebted to it for the initiation it has provided into the wonders of bird life.

Unlike many works written to meet a particular need which age very quickly, this book has retained its freshness and remains, now as then, the best introduction to bird biology. Even so, the studies which have appeared in the course of the last two decades are numerous, and, in order to enable this fine book to pursue its educational purpose, it was desirable that the original text should be brought up to date. This the author has done magnificently: without burdening his account with an undue mass of detail, he has succeeded in distilling the quintessence of those observations and experiences which provide a general and durable interest. The illustrative material has been greatly enriched, taking advantage of the considerable progress that has been achieved in colour photography.

Thus rejuvenated, Birds of the World *can now continue to give the younger generation of nature lovers the same stimulus which the first edition supplied for their elders.*

François BOURLIÈRE

Department of Physiology
Université René Descartes, Paris.

TRANSLATOR'S NOTE TO THE FIRST EDITION

In making this translation for British and American readers I have kept as closely as possible to the original French text but, in agreement with the author, a few small modifications have been made. I have adopted the vernacular names of birds most commonly used by British authors, but where necessary American equivalents have been inserted [in square brackets].

The classification in the original French conformed with that used by J. Berlioz in the volume on birds in the recent French "Traité de Zoologie" but it has been altered to meet the wishes of American systematists.

Phyllis BARCLAY-SMITH

INTRODUCTION

The study of birds, like that of any zoological group, can be undertaken advantageously from various angles. Specialists are perhaps not always in agreement as to the relative importance which should be given to the various branches of this subject, but it is certain that for the amateur observer it is the life of the bird, as it is enacted before our eyes, which offers the greatest attraction.

Such studies have today become very important, and it is for this reason that the present work is devoted simply to the description of bird behaviour and related questions. One such question—the effect of human agency on bird populations—is too far-ranging for it to be treated in detail in this work, since it is linked with too many problems of a general character for any satisfactory exposition of the lengthy arguments involved to be given here; on this subject we shall therefore confine ourselves to occasional references.

Even though many of the facts presented are accessible to any attentive observer, this does not mean other branches of ornithology are without interest; in addition to the descriptive sciences such as anatomy, others such as systematics—the study of classification—or geographical distribution, raise questions of great importance which are allied to wider problems such as evolution.

These subjects are difficult to summarise in a concrete manner, for to appreciate their value it is necessary to have a full knowledge of many kinds of birds, which in practice can only be acquired by access to large collections. It should be mentioned in this connection that in modern ornithology the era of forming private collections of local birds, which was once fashionable, is now very largely a thing of the past. The public collections in museums will always maintain their educational value, but only by the study of long series of specimens from different regions, which constitute the study collections of the larger zoological institutions, can a full knowledge of the subject be obtained.

A review, even very condensed, of the Class Birds is not possible here; however, in order to obtain a better understanding of their characteristics, before dealing with the study of their habits, a brief account of the principles on which their classification is based does not seem out of place.

In the whole animal kingdom there is probably no other important group which is so homogeneous as that of birds, nor one in which it is so difficult to establish sub-divisions. If the differences in general structure in mammals are considered, such as those between a monkey, bat, stag and whale, for example, or between a snake and a turtle, in reptiles, to mention only the vertebrates, it must be admitted that nothing analogous is found in birds. It is comparatively easy to separate off a few well-defined groups, but the very great majority of species only differ in secondary characters; the resemblances, which are often due to the convergence of superficial characters, have not the importance that they appear to have at first sight.

In order to establish natural divisions it is essential to take into account the combination of all the characteristics of the species under consideration, including not only external morphology, but also anatomy and biology. It is very often only by numerous and comprehensive comparisons that it is possible to decide the position of a species or of a group, and this is why the study of the classification of birds, and the general approach which it necessitates, can provide such great interest. It should be mentioned that the very small number of fossil remains which has been collected does not make it possible to obtain from palaeontology the valuable aid which it brings to the study of mammals.

The older naturalists, who had the merit of making serious attempts to establish a natural classification, did not possess sufficient facts for an accurate general understanding of the bird-world; and their classifications, based mainly on European species, cannot be adapted to the multitude of forms since described. Following the example of Linnaeus, Buffon, Cuvier and their disciples, in too many elementary treatises the practice was maintained in several countries of dividing birds into a few large Orders, birds of prey, passeres, climbers, gallinaceous birds, waders and palmipeds, groupings based on very badly defined external characters. For example the classing together of Moorhen and Heron in the waders, and Penguin and Gull in the palmipeds, shows to what extent these divisions are arbitrary. These first attempts were very useful at the time, but it was not possible to maintain them.

The homogeneity of the Class Birds has resulted in its division into a considerable number of Orders, which is, it must be admitted, slightly confusing for the amateur. In order to define them it has been necessary to take into consideration characters which may seem to have little importance in themselves, such as the arrangement of the tendons of the toes, or of the bones of the palate, but their study shows that they indicate closer affinities than more obvious characteristics. Further, certain details, both morphological and biological, which are important in one series, may have much less significance in another.

The result of this state of affairs reflects the nature of the birds themselves in that any group, however well defined, always shows more or less common features with several others; the choices which it is necessary to make to place them in a linear series—an

Group of Ostriches, East Africa.

Whiskered Tern on nest. ▶

Young Cassowary. Cassowaries, which feed mainly on fruit, represent the Ratites in the tropical forests of New Guinea and northern Australia.

King Penguins. The picture shows clearly the paddle-like shape of the flipper, characteristic of the Impennes.

Among Carinates, the difference in size between species is considerable. Besides very large birds such as Marabou Storks (below) and the Jabiru Stork (lower right) there are also found the smallest of all, the Humming Birds (opposite).

extremely arbitrary operation but in practice indispensable—must always be regarded as debatable. According to the relative importance which is attached to one character or another the groups are differently placed in the series and the details of classification change frequently from one author to another.

There is more or less agreement that birds should be divided into three large, but very artificial divisions:

RATITES, birds with non-functional wings, lacking a keel on the breastbone; some authors include Tinamous in this division;

IMPENNES, with wings transformed into flippers;

CARINATES, in which the wings are normal (very rarely atrophied), with a developed keel.

The first group includes the Ostriches, Cassowaries, etc., and the Kiwi, the second the Penguins, and the third comprises all the rest. This represents a variable number of species depending on whether or not certain local races are granted this status. The generally accepted figure is about 8,500, of which 5,000 are Passerines. This vast mass is divided into Orders which are very unequal so far as numbers of species are concerned, but equal in theoretical importance, and each Order is sub-divided into a varying number of Families. For simplification a summarised list of these is given in an appendix at the end of this book; the less important groups have been omitted except when some particular characteristic necessitates reference to them in the text.

It is well known that each species, whether animal or vegetable, has an international scientific name composed of two latinised words, one denoting the genus and the other the species (here the designation of "subspecies" which requires a third word will not be taken into consideration). Although these names are in common use for many plants (Geranium, Begonia, Crocus, etc.) in the case of animals it is customary only to use them in technical publications. An index of the birds referred to is given at the end of the book.

The author cannot conclude this introduction without thanking Professor F. Bourlière for his kindness in reading the manuscript of this work and for many useful improvements he has suggested.

Tawny Owl alighting at nest-hole: the arrangement of the wing-slots due to the sudden contraction of the flight feathers is clearly visible on the right wing.

Kittiwake in very slow gliding flight. The bastard wing, a small tuft of separate feathers seen at the angle of the wing, is lifted to guide the air flow and prevent eddies on the upper surface. The wings and sides of the tail are raised and the feet lowered in order to increase stability of flight.

Chapter I
DAILY ACTIVITIES

The daily rhythm

The daily rhythm in the activity of birds, whether they are diurnal or nocturnal, follows more or less exactly the variations in the amount of daylight. The diurnal birds regulate their waking by the sunrise and their going to sleep by the dusk, but with displacements varying according to species. Larks, Redstarts and Woodpeckers begin their activities very early, Starlings and House-Sparrows are later and in general the birds which wake early remain awake later in the evening than the others.

It seems that the sense of vision controls the periods of activity of birds. We know that the majority are diurnal but nocturnal species occur in many groups. In addition to the Owls, some of which moreover hunt more or less regularly during the day (Pigmy Owl, Hawk-Owl), there are the Nightjars, the Bat-eating Buzzard of Africa, a New Zealand Parrot, the Stone Curlew, and some Herons such as the Night Heron.

There are some exceptions to this rule; a number of species such as Flamingos and certain Ducks, which do not appear to have any preference, like the shore-birds, follow the rhythm of the tides, because of the exigencies of their food requirements.

During migration many diurnal birds move at night, generally during the early hours, and at nesting time the Shearwaters which are habitually more or less active by day become strictly nocturnal.

During the course of the day the bird's activity is not at all uniform, but it seeks its food chiefly in the morning soon after waking up, and it is then also that it sings most and the main acts of reproduction, such as courtship displays, laying, etc., take place. There is usually a period of rest in the middle of the day and a resumption of activity in the evening. In winter when the days are short the rest during the day is suppressed; in high latitudes the search for food may even begin before dawn and end after dusk if the length of daylight is too short for the bird to get sufficient food.

The duration of sleep depends on the length of the night. In the arctic summer, however, when the sun remains continually above the horizon, the birds neverthe-less go to sleep for a few hours, generally before midnight.

The most frequent position of a sleeping bird is well known, the head turned backwards with the beak buried in the feathers of the back. The perching birds settle in such a way that the toes, by a special arrangement of the tendons, automatically cling to the branches; others sleep standing on one leg, while some sleep lying on the ground; Penguins sleep standing up, the beak under one flipper and the feet turned up with the heels only touching the ground.

Many birds sleep in the open, sometimes congregating in flocks on certain trees or reed beds. The winter sleeping quarters of Rooks and Starlings where all the individuals from a given region congregate every evening are well known. When there is an exceptional migration the number of Bramblings congregating each evening in the same forest of central Switzerland has been estimated at 70 million. These migratory flocks may extend for nearly twenty miles and be over 200 yards wide. Some birds sleep in holes in trees which some species

bore out for themselves. Certain Woodpeckers make a sleeping chamber for the winter similar to the hole which they make for their nest and some small Parrakeets sleep hanging head down from a branch. Swifts sometimes spend the entire night in flight.

During sleep metabolism is slightly lowered but not to any great extent except in the Humming Birds and perhaps some other species. Their metabolism drops considerably during the night and their internal temperature which is usually about 100°–104° F may fall as low as 64°–68° F; on waking the return to normal is very rapid. This is more than simple sleep, it is a veritable state of lethargy somewhat resembling that of hibernating animals. The same phenomenon has also been observed in the diurnal sleep of bats. It diminishes the loss of heat in these small species which, proportionately to their weight, grow cold more quickly than the others.

A flock of Starlings settling for the night. Many of them, birds of the year, are still in their juvenile light-brown unspotted plumage.

Locomotion

The terrestrial locomotion of birds is always very simple, as they only have a single pair of carrying limbs, which does not allow the varied combinations that exist in mammals. The species with long legs walk or run, some small birds do the same, but the majority progress by hopping. In certain birds (Larks, Pipits, Wagtails) in which walking is the normal gait of the adult, the young have been observed to begin by hopping.

When the legs are set very far back, as in the birds which are good swimmers, walking becomes difficult. It may even be practically impossible, as in the case of the Divers [Loons] which hardly ever come on land except to nest, and wriggle along on their stomachs. This position is sometimes assumed by Penguins, which, although they frequently walk upright, are able to progress in this position with the help of their flippers. As for Swifts, they scarcely ever come to ground, their toes enabling them only to cling to vertical surfaces.

There are few marked adaptations of the feet of birds that walk; those which move about on unstable ground have comparatively long toes, very long in the Rails, and above all in the Jacanas which are able to walk about on floating vegetation. Species in sandy regions generally have short and thick toes, even joined together in certain Sand-Grouse. The Ostrich has only two, very unequal in size. The toes of Grouse are edged on each side with long scales which form a sort of comb and increase the supporting surface on snow.

When moving about in trees birds usually hop. Parrots climb with the aid of their beaks. A number of small birds cling to the bark; thus Nuthatches easily move about in all directions on the trunks and branches of trees. The Woodpeckers have a tail composed of extremely stiff feathers, rough at the tips, which gives them a solid support. They always ascend by vertical hops and when by chance they descend by the same method they maintain the same attitude, the tail being raised before each backward jump. The Creepers and Woodhewers, whose tails are of the same type, move about in the same way.

A bird floating on the water swims by making simultaneous or successive pushes with its feet, which when folded back offer little resistance to forward movement. The webbed feet of the Anatidae, Gulls, etc., are well known; Coots, Grebes and some other species do not have a complete web, but independent webs on each toe.

When a bird floating on the water prepares to dive, it increases its density by exhaling the air from the pneumatic sacs which form part of its respiratory system and by compressing its plumage which, likewise, retains a good deal of air. It must, however, overcome the upward force; it is most often only the feet—situated very far back in the good divers—that are used as a means of propulsion, the wings remaining closed and partly covered by the flank feathers. In certain Ducks (Eider, Long-tailed Duck [Old Squaw], Velvet Scoter) the wings remain folded, but held away from the body, and their movement helps progression; it is curious that in these birds the bastard wing (the thumb and the feathers it carries) is usually held

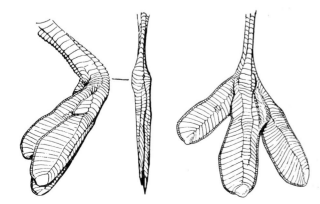

Foot of Great Crested Grebe; folded during forward movement in water (side view, front view); spread during backward movement (front view).

comparatively easily. Nevertheless in the case of flapping flight,
in particular, there are still points
which remain obscure. It should
not be forgotten that although
the laws which govern the regular
movement of a surface in a fluid
are well known, there is still no
precise knowledge about variable
movements such as the alternating action of a bird's wing, the
complex form and irregularities
of which increase the difficulties
of the problem, and the aero-
dynamic properties of small wings
are still unknown.

Gliding flight is the simplest
and almost all birds use it at least
occasionally; with wings extended and motionless they let themselves glide in the air, but it is
evident that in calm air this must
be a descending movement as
there is no propulsive effort.

In soaring flight, on the contrary, although the birds do not
supply any more propulsive effort,
they appear to be able to guide

in a very different position from
the normal. In the Auks (Razorbills, Guillemots, etc.) it is the
wings only which play an active
part, the feet serving as a rudder.
It is the same in the Penguins
where the wings are, as is well
known, transformed into organs
specially adapted to this type of

swimming which is a kind of
underwater "flight".

The mechanism of bird flight
has long remained a mystery. At
the present time the progress
of aerodynamics, itself resulting
partly in the beginning from the
study of birds, makes it possible
to explain certain phenomena

Ducks diving
Tufted Duck   *Velvet Scoter*

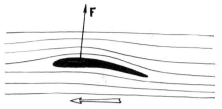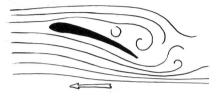

*Flow of air round wing which is moving
from right to left
left: normal incidence; F=resultant force;
right: too great an incidence*

themselves at will. Some can glide in calm air with very little loss of altitude, only a few inches a second; now it is not uncommon for air to have rising currents of the same magnitude; under these conditions the loss of altitude is compensated and the bird flies horizontally; if the rising air is of sufficient force it gains height without any effort. It is the same phenomenon which is used by gliders for soaring flight.

Although the action of the wind on the contour of the earth's surface is not negligible, it is principally the heating of the soil, varying according to local conditions, which produces rising columns of hot air separated by zones of calm or descending air. The bird circles round in order to remain in a favourable zone

where it gains height, then glides to another where the process is repeated and thus great distances may be covered without any wing-beats. This is the type of flight frequently used by birds of prey, chiefly during their migrations.

Certain birds can also fly without wing-beats, where there is no rising air current, by utilising the variations of wind velocity. It is known that in practice the movement of the air is never uniform; if the bird advances in the same direction as the wind and this slackens, the bird's inertia will partly maintain its speed; for a certain time therefore it will advance more quickly in relation to the surrounding air, and, by making the necessary adjustments to the incidence of its wings, will be able to gain height. If it is

advancing against the wind it will utilise the accelerations in the same way. The bird, which certainly feels the slightest air currents, regulates its own movements accordingly, but direct observation is difficult.

During flight without wing-beats the bird does not use its own energy, but nevertheless it experiences muscular fatigue as the wings must remain horizontal despite the air pressure which balances its weight and tends to raise the wings.

The mechanism of flapping flight, although varying in detail from one type of bird to another, can be explained diagrammatically in the following way; it is known that if a surface is displaced while making a slight angle to the direction of its movement, the action of the air works in such a way as to produce a force perpendicular to the surface in question. This force increases with the angle of incidence and suddenly drops when this reaches a certain degree. When the bird's wing is

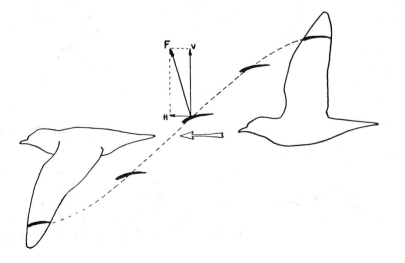

*Effect of air on a part of the wing during
the down-stroke. F=resultant force;
V=vertical component; H=horizontal
component.*

Puffin about to land. The feet, replacing the too short tail, serve as rudders.

lowered, each of its components describes a trajectory oblique to the direction of the body; the slant of the wing with this trajectory is such that the resultant force is directed upwards and forwards. The vertical component of this force counterbalances the weight of the bird and the horizontal component makes it advance. It is therefore not a backward sculling movement but the forward movement of the wing which makes the bird advance.

It must be pointed out that because of the variation in the angles of the trajectories of the different components, a certain amount of twisting of the wing is necessary. The extremity of the wing plays, to some extent, the part of a propeller, the base that of lift force.

In upward motion the wing is more or less folded. The large feathers rise in tiers like slats in a shutter, thus reducing resistance, and the bird rises, through the agency of the air, without appreciably consuming or producing

energy. However, in certain circumstances, the wing, acting by means of its dorsal power, may contribute to the propulsive movement.

It is not possible to examine in detail the bird's adaptations from flight in general to various special types of flight in particular. The simple examination of a wing is enough to show how lightly it is constructed; the bones themselves are often hollow, which augments their resistance without increasing their weight and the whole wing possesses very great strength with little inertia. The surface of the wing is not flat, but curved with the concavity below; in addition the arrangement of the bones and the wing-coverts makes the front edge much thicker. Experience has shown that this form of wing has far greater efficiency than one with a flat surface.

Although there is a fairly definite general rule, each form of wing is so well adapted to a particular type of flight that in spite of our very superficial knowledge, it is possible to make conjectures as to the behaviour of the bird itself by examination of the wing.

Among the birds which are good gliders two categories can be clearly distinguished; sea birds and land birds. The first have long, narrow pointed wings, the maximum length being found in

Whinchat brakes when about to alight by spreading the wings and tail to full extent.

Blue Tit: maximum extension of the down-stroke of the wing.

the Albatrosses. The bird can glide at a slight angle and readily vary its speed. It easily maintains its height in the rising currents such as those formed on the slopes of waves, and from this point of view the flight of Shearwaters passing from one crest to another, changing their inclination while remaining level with the water, is very characteristic. Gulls are also frequently seen following a ship with motionless wings; they have found a rising current caused by the ship's wash and are kept up in the air somewhat like a ball on a jet of water. Small species have not always sufficient wing surfaces to be able to glide in all circumstances; the length and narrowness of their wings allow considerable twisting, very variable in different phases of the wing-beat, which accounts for the characteristic flexibility of the movement of the tips of the wings of Gulls.

The large gliding land birds have a much shorter wing of more uniform breadth which makes it possible for them to glide very gently and, by utilising the slight rising currents of warm air, easily to maintain height in relatively calm air. This type of wing shows to a marked degree an arrangement which is found, in varying degrees, in many birds: the large feathers at the tip of the wing separate like the fingers of a hand and by sudden constrictions increase the spaces between them. This arrangement seems to be adapted for several purposes such as reduction of the lateral eddies which have a tendency to form at the tip of the wing as a result of the difference of pressure between the upper and lower surface, for currents are not produced on a pointed, tapering wing; and guiding of the air under a larger, and therefore more favourable, angle of incidence, by this combination of narrow surfaces, which become distorted under air pressure. In order to produce these effects the feathers must not be too far apart, and there is a locking arrangement which automatically limits their separation.

Common Heron braking as it lands. The currents which form above the wing have the effect of raising the wing coverts.

During flight Flamingos keep their necks stretched forward to counterbalance the weight of the very long extended feet behind. ▶

King Penguin swimming on the surface, its flippers outstretched for this aquatic "flight".

The *American Purple Gallinule* walking on floating vegetation (Florida). Its long toes enable it to move with ease over this unstable support.

Tree-creeper on a vertical trunk. Tail-support is common among Woodpeckers, and also among the Wood-creepers of tropical America.

Golden Eagle leaving nest. It could be claimed that the bird is almost in normal flight from the moment of take-off. In the case of the Whooper Swan, however, take-off is a complicated procedure: it needs to run along the surface of the water until it gains the necessary momentum.

Spoonbills returning to their nests. The descent is made in level flight. As the bird is about to alight the body is lifted for braking and the legs are stretched forward to grip the branches.

Lesser Pied Kingfisher hovering before diving into the water. Such hovering, familiar among various birds of prey in many parts of the world, is also typical of certain Kingfishers which hunt their prey in the same way.

characteristic type of flight by which it can often be identified. Small birds do not usually have continuous wing-beats; a series of beats is followed by a period of rest during which the bird advances as a result of its acquired speed. It then loses height, which is regained by a further series of wing-beats and thus the line of flight undulates in a characteristic manner. Many Woodpeckers, which fly in this way, completely close their wings during the descents. Though the necessary effort must on the average be the same as for continuous flight, the muscular fatigue is certainly less. The large Falcons also sometimes fly in the same way, but their ability as gliders enables them to glide on outspread wings during the periods of rest without appreciable loss of height or speed.

Peculiarities of this kind are innumerable. Among other examples in the large Falcons may be pointed out the diving descent with closed wings, often followed by rapid ascent on motionless wings. The speed which the bird can reach in these dives is very considerable, and it seems that the highest speed ever recorded for a bird has been in the stoop of the Peregrine—175 miles an hour.

Nightjar taking off; the left wing is reversed and working through its upper surface; probably the bird turns while rising vertically.

The speeds of flight vary in different species and it might be tempting to try to estimate the strength of a bird by the measurements given but it must not be forgotten that the circumstances in which they are carried out are not always comparable: the maximum speed of a bird when pursued, the cruising speed on a long distance, etc.; also it is not always known exactly if it was possible to eliminate the influence of the wind correctly. But even without taking into account certain rash estimates, it is obvious that the speed, even of birds which are not very strong, is considerable.

In their usual movements small birds fly at about 25 miles an hour; the hunting flight of Swallows and Swifts, which appears very rapid because of its flexibility, has a speed of the same order; Swifts, nevertheless, attain a speed of 60 miles an hour in certain circumstances, a speed rarely reached by birds. The following are examples of normal speeds: Geese and Ducks 45–50 miles per hour, reaching 70 miles per hour when pursued; 25–37½ in gallinaceous birds; 25–50 in the small waders; 20–30 in Gulls; 30–45 in Pigeons; and 45–50, and perhaps more, in Humming Birds.

It would also be interesting to know the acceleration of which a bird is capable, but it does not ever seem to have been measured.

The direction of flight is attained by visual means even by nocturnal birds whose eyes are sensitive to very low intensities of light. But the Oil-Bird and the Salanganes [Collocalia] which nest in caves which are completely dark appear to avoid obstacles in the same way as bats, by means of the echoes caused by a cry which they utter at regular intervals. This use of a sonar system may be compared to that employed in diving by certain creatures—Penguins in particular—when hunting for their prey.

Stork alighting at nest. By means of different actions by the wings, the trajectory obtains the necessary precision for landing on the nest.

Food

If a review of the foods of birds were made it would be necessary to draw up a list of practically everything edible on the face of the globe. Though certain birds have a definite, and sometimes very strict, diet, there are others whose tastes or needs are more varied and who change their diet according to circumstances, and even according to locality. It is therefore impossible to deal here with so vast a subject and only general habits can be described.

Among vegetable foods, fruit and seeds are the most generally eaten. It is well known how many small passerine birds search for the seeds of various plants, but many birds of all sizes, such as Pigeons, gallinaceous birds and Parrots, also eat them.

The seeds of conifers, especially in cold regions, are sometimes the sole food of such birds as Crossbills or Pine Grosbeaks. Nuts, almonds and other hard fruits are only consumed by birds with beaks sufficiently strong to crack them, such as the Corvidae and Parrots; Woodpeckers and Nuthatches wedge them in a fork of a branch, or crevice in the bark, and then hammer them

open with their beaks. Nut-crackers and Jays, among others, have the habit of collecting them and making stores.

Fruits are particularly sought after; in tropical forests their ripening at various times causes

more or less regular movements of the birds which feed on them. Certain kinds of Pigeons such as the Green Pigeons and Fruit Pigeons live on them exclusively; Toucans, Trogons, Touracos, various Parrots, Hornbills, and

Black Woodpecker at nest-hole in the usual position of Woodpeckers, supported by the tail.

Barn Owl bringing a field-mouse to the nest.

subsist on organic matter found in water and mud.

The animal food taken is also very varied. As is well known the numerous nocturnal and diurnal birds of prey capture mammals and birds; the Corvidae, Ardeidae (Herons) and Storks (Ciconiidae), and even quite small passerine birds like the Shrikes, do likewise. To the majority of species it is the small rodents which pay the heaviest toll. Nests are robbed by certain Corvidae, Gulls and Skuas and in Malaysia there is a large Eagle which feeds mainly on eggs. Some birds of prey like the Short-toed Eagle of Europe, or the Secretary Bird of the grassland regions of Africa, take reptiles, but many birds of all kinds eat small reptiles and batrachians when they can get them; in North Africa Clot Bey's Lark frequently eats lizards.

Fruit-eating birds:
a) *Blue-naped Mouse-bird* (Colius macrourus), *West Africa;* b) *Spot-billed Toucanet* (*female*) (Selenidera maculirostris), *Brazil;* c) *Pink-necked Fruit-Dove* (Ptilinopus porphyreus), *Java, Sumatra;* d) *Masked Trogon* (Trogon personatus), *tropical America;* e) *Lesser Green Leaf-bird* (Chloropsis cyanopogon), *Malaysia.* ▶

many others consume large quantities; it is well known how in Europe certain fruits, even dried up in winter, attract small birds. They are also eaten by birds whose normal diet is very different, as for example certain birds of prey, among others the Vulturine Fish-Eagle of Equatorial Africa, which has adapted itself to the fruits of the oil palm. The Oil-Bird, a South American nocturnal bird closely allied to the Nightjars and the only nocturnal fruit-eating bird, gathers fruit from the ends of branches.

Humming Birds, Sunbirds, Honey-eaters and certain Parrots search for the nectar of flowers. Some Woodpeckers extract sap from trees. Swans and Geese graze on grass and the Black Geese sometimes add algae to their menu. Grouse eat many leaves and buds, and the Red Grouse of Scotland lives almost entirely on the young shoots of heather. Land or aquatic tubers, bulbs, and rhizomes are consumed by the most diverse species, varying from Moorhens [Gallinules] to Parrots—in New Guinea there is a Parrot which seems to eat nothing but fungi. Flamingos

Scarlet-chested Sunbird on the flower-head of an aloe. The birds in this group visit flowers not only for their nectar but also for the numerous small insects attracted to the blooms.

Scissorbill fishing. This species skims over the water with its lower mandible regularly immersed.

Africa: a gathering of Vultures round a carcase.

Like the Sunbird, this Humming Bird (the Rufous-tailed Humming Bird, of Brazil) seeks nectar, but the precision of its flight enables it to do so while hovering in front of the flowers.

Cattle Egret searching for insects disturbed by cattle (Andalusia).

Von der Decken's Hornbill (East Africa), one of the numerous species of small Hornbills inhabiting Asia and more especially Africa which feed mainly on fruit.

European Bee-eater. This bird has a natural immunity against the poison of the Hymenoptera, which provide its chief source of food.

The Vultures, which have weak claws, feed on carcases, but many other diurnal birds of prey, such as Eagles, Kites, etc., who can capture their prey alive do not disdain carrion. The Corvidae do the same and in maritime areas very many birds live on dead matter of all kinds thrown up by the sea (Gulls, Skuas, Sheathbills) or floating on it (Petrels, Albatrosses).

Fish form the food, often exclusively, of many water birds such as Pelicans, Gannets, Terns, Grebes, Divers [Loons], Sawbills, etc., but a number of land birds also feed on fish, such as Ospreys, Kites, and various noc-

turnal birds of prey like the Fish-Owl of tropical Asia.

Of all the invertebrates, insects are those most generally consumed by land birds of all kinds. Many birds have an exclusively insectivorous diet which may even be very specialised; such as the

Swallows, Swifts and Nightjars which feed on flying insects. The Flycatchers also pursue flying insects but occasionally also take others. A good number of birds of prey, especially the smaller ones, eat insects taken either from the ground or on the wing.

Puffin returning to nest with sand-eels held crosswise in its beak.

Types of exotic birds with specialised bills: a) *Ivory-billed Woodpecker* (Campephilus principalis), *North America;* b) *Green-billed Toucan* (Ramphastos dicolorus), *Brazil;* c) *Bearded Barbet* (Lybius dubius), *West Africa;* d) *Great-billed Parrakeet* (Tanygnathus megalorhynchus), *Moluccas;* e) *Large Frogmouth* (Batrachostomus auritus), *Malaysia;* f) *Red-billed Sickle-bill* (Campylorhamphus trochilirostris), *Brazil;* g) *Scarlet Ibis* (Guara rubra), *tropical America;* h) *Sword-bill Humming Bird* (Ensifera ensifera), *Colombia;* i) *Hook-billed Kingfisher* (Melidora macrorhina), *New Guinea.*

Woodpeckers search for the larvae found in bark or wood and very often also consume large quantities of ants. In Africa, Honeyguides live entirely on the larvae of bees and honey, which they take when the bees' nest is more or less destroyed by other animals or man; their calls indicate the position of the wild bees' nests, hence their name. Cuckoos eat caterpillars, even those with irritating hairs. Many small birds, Tits, Warblers, etc., take any insects they can get; and in winter the Blue Tit actively searches for those hidden in the dry rushes of the marshes.

Land snails are eaten by birds such as Thrushes, which swallow them whole if they are small, or first break the shell on a stone. An American bird of prey, the Snail Hawk, lives almost entirely on a large aquatic snail. The bivalve molluscs are taken by Oyster-catchers, certain Storks, which prise them open, and by Ducks such as Eiders and Scoters, which swallow them whole. Gulls drop molluscs, whose shells are too hard for their beaks, from a height in order to break them. Many sea birds eat cephalopods, cuttle-fish, squids, etc., especially when they come to the surface at night, and many other kinds of plankton. Even the Coelenterates such as Medusae and Physalia, whose stinging characteristics are very acute, are eaten by some Petrels and Albatrosses.

Finally, mention should be made of the worms and other small animals with soft bodies which live in the sand on beaches, mud, or marshy ground, and which constitute a large part of the food of shore birds and certain species of land birds.

Many birds have a very varied diet; the large Corvidae, for example, eat almost anything. Often the variations in diet arise from

Tracks left by Flamingos when feeding. Trampling round and round in one place the birds dig up the mud with their beaks, the filtering lamellae retain any organic matter, and basin-like depressions are left behind.

Avocets take their food either at surface level by means of lateral movements of the beak or by sweeping on the bottom.

the availability of food at different seasons. The small passerine birds of Europe are characteristic from this point of view, even seed-eaters capture insects in summer, at least for feeding their young, and the few insectivorous birds that remain for the winter have to content themselves with vegetable food at this season.

The Honey-Buzzard is a bird of prey whose food mainly consists of wasps, bumble-bees, and more especially their brood-combs. When they arrive in

A pair of Honey-Buzzards at the nest. One of them carries a piece of cone from a wasps' nest.

spring the colonies of hymenoptera are still only small and the birds therefore temporarily adopt the same food as other raptors—rodents, reptiles and various insects. At the end of the summer, berries are added to their menu.

In the summer months the Little Owl feeds mainly on insects but in winter its diet is the same as that of its near relatives, and many other examples of the same kind could be quoted. It seems that in certain circumstances at any rate, the bird may have adapted itself to these periodic changes of diet to such an extent that the seasonal preferences have become instinctive. Young birds like Curlews and Black-headed Gulls, when reared in captivity, will only accept the food which is habitually taken by these birds at the same period.

Exceptional circumstances may cause birds to take to unusual feeding habits. For instance during a very hard winter Magpies and Crows have been known to peck cattle in order to eat the flesh. This has become a regular habit with a New Zealand Parrot —the Kea—which used to feed on vegetable matter, insects and occasionally on carcases, but now attacks living sheep.

(European) Sparrow-Hawk. A lightly built, not very powerful, bird of prey whose great speed enables it to catch small birds unawares.

The bird's choice of food depends on an instinctive taste expressive of a certain physiological adaptation and also the physical possibilities it has for obtaining it. From the latter point of view the methods of pursuit of birds of prey are characteristic. The Peregrine Falcon, which has a rapid and sustained flight, catches its prey in flight; the small Hobby, which is particularly agile, frequently pursues insects such as dragon-flies, which are too fast for other birds. The European Sparrow-Hawk, whose flight is rapid, capable of sharp turns, but not sustained, takes birds by surprise while they are perching. The Buzzards, which have a heavy

Types of beaks of birds of prey:
Left: Peregrine Falcon
Right: Bateleur Eagle

flight, mark down rodents from a slightly elevated perch; the Kites, unable to turn rapidly, mostly content themselves with dead animals, or sick fish floating on the surface of the water.

It is not only the ability of movement which influences the choice of food; various morphological characteristics such as the long neck with sharp movements of the Herons or Snake-birds, can be of great importance; similarly the shape of the beak, which varies so greatly in birds, may determine the character of the food. Among European birds the Crossbill is a classic example, the arrangement of its mandibles, which is unique in the avian world, enabling it to tear apart the scales of the pine and fir cones and extract the seeds. Other birds eat these seeds, but except for the Woodpeckers whose powerful beaks are able to demolish the cones, they cannot get at them unless dryness has caused the scales to open; the Crossbill can do this at any time and therefore can live in the forest in winter. The beaks of the Woodpeckers form a vertically cutting chisel at the tip, but their most remarkable characteristic is the tongue. This is extremely long and the hinder end lies at rest behind the skull and comes forward along the beak or round the right eye. The very pointed tip with its tactile papillae can search for insects in the depths of their galleries.

Immature American Bald Eagle.

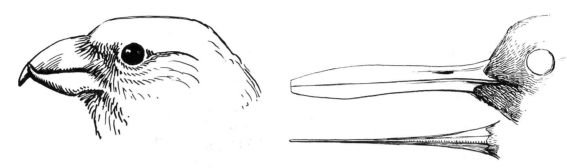

Left: Crossbill;
Right: Beak of
Oystercatcher
(side view and
from above)

The tongue of nectar-eating birds (Humming Birds, Sunbirds, etc.) is grooved or even tube-like, which enables them to suck up nectar. That of the Lories, Parrots specialised for the same kind of food, has a sort of brush at the tip. In Parrots, however, the tongue is a very delicate tactile organ and it is always curious to see with what delicacy these birds with enormous and powerful beaks like the Cockatoos use it to pick out their food.

Numerous very specialised adaptations could be mentioned such as the knife-like bill of the Oystercatcher which enables it to prise open bivalve molluscs, the supple and sensitive bill of the Woodcock, which finds worms in soft ground, the long, more or less curved beaks of the Creepers, or Woodhewers of tropical America, which explore crevices in bark, the beaks with filtering lamellae of the Anatidae and Flamingos, etc.,

The special shape of the bill of Spoonbills is not found to the same marked degree in any other bird. When searching for food the bill is kept half open and plunged almost vertically into the water while the head is moved from side to side in a scything motion to sift the food from the water.

but it must be pointed out that if a high specialisation enables a bird to obtain special food, it can also take other foods, and it is quite exceptional that its diet should be exclusive. The Humming Birds and Sunbirds eat many small insects, the Nightjars gather food from the ground and as already mentioned certain birds of prey have been known to eat fruit. It can even be that a beak is never used for the kind of food for which it appears primarily specialised; this is the case in the

Dark-backed Weaver which like the other Weavers has the large beak of the seed-eater but only eats insects.

The birds' methods of feeding by assuring the dissemination of seeds in certain cases, are not without importance in relation to vegetation. Seeds can stick to the feet of birds and be carried a long way, or forgotten in their hiding-places, etc., but principally they are ejected after passing through the digestive tract; but they do not lose their power of

germination during this process and for some it even seems necessary for their development.

The part played by birds in fertilising flowers is sometimes important, particularly in the case of nectar-eating birds. The flower is not always specially adapted to this method of pollination and insects also play their part. On the other hand, in certain cases the conformation of the flower is such that only the bird can suck the nectar. In doing so, a mechanism is unleashed which causes the pollen to adhere to the bird's forehead and so be transported from one flower to another.

The effect on human activities of food taken by birds is a subject on which the observation of occasional facts and hasty generalisations have most often presented the facts of the problem in a wrong light. It must be recognised that, though a fairly general idea of the food of a bird can be obtained, it is actually impossible to know the details, except in rare cases. Direct observation only gives a very small part of the necessary knowledge.

The analysis of stomach contents, quite interesting though this may be, can only give incomplete results; certain foods such as seeds and the hard parts of insects remain identifiable for

The Short-toed, or Snake, Eagle, is a large bird of prey with weak claws, which feeds almost entirely on reptiles. Snakes are brought to the nest half swallowed, the tail hanging out of the bird's beak. In the centre photograph, a fully grown youngster pulls a viper from its parent's throat.

quite a long time, but others such as soft insects, larvae, etc., are rapidly unrecognisable under the action of the digestive juices which continues even after the death of the bird. The analysis of the pellets of Owls is almost the only case which gives definite results. It is known that these birds swallow their prey whole and that the indigestible matter such as hair and bones is ejected in the form of pellets which can easily be collected from near their habitual perching places; by the examination of the remains of bones the nature of their prey can easily be determined. Many other birds regurgitate debris in the same way, but in smaller quantities and not in a fit condition to be of use. The remains of food under the perching places of diurnal birds of prey give some indication of their diet.

African Black Heron fishing. When this little heron spots a fish it spreads its wings and hides under them in order to catch it.

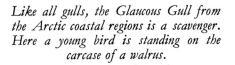

Like all gulls, the Glaucous Gull from the Arctic coastal regions is a scavenger. Here a young bird is standing on the carcase of a walrus.

Little Owl carrying a young field-mouse.

It is therefore impossible to estimate the balance of influences exercised by birds and no conclusion can be drawn from a few isolated observations. All birds of prey should not be condemned because a Goshawk is seen taking a Partridge or fowl from time to time; and the Goshawk itself by rights should not be blamed, because of the good it does in destroying the Corvidae. It should also not be forgotten that the predators keep down the spread of epidemics by the destruction of sickly animals; for example, cases are known where the destruction of Eagles was followed by the disappearance of chamois. Very often the same species appears "useful" in some circumstances and "harmful" in others and though it may appear for example that, from a general point of view, the presence of birds of prey which feed on rodents can only have a beneficial effect on an agricultural country, actually the economic value of the species cannot, in general, be exactly determined. What is certain is that so long as man does not interfere there is an all-round satisfactory equilibrium. As a result of agricultural activities in particular, this equilibrium may be partly modified, but it is evidently essential not to take any action of which it is impossible to foresee the consequences. In this sphere —as in many others—the best is the enemy of the good.

The Kingfisher feeds not only on fish but also on any small water creatures it can catch. ▶

The Brahminy Kite is a fish-hawk of the tropics, its range extending from India to northern Australia; it is especially partial to diseased and dead fish.

Kea, a peculiar Parrot of South Island, New Zealand, whose carnivorous habits are unique in this group of birds.

Two Hildebrandt Starlings (a young bird being fed by an adult) and two Black-headed Weavers take advantage of the food offered to them (East Africa). Behind them is an agama.

Dunlin roosting; though not asleep they adopt the sleeping posture.

Various activities

The time taken by a bird in searching for food varies considerably, depending mainly on its abundance, but there are always periods of rest when a great part of the time is spent in preening, which is done with great care. It is while arranging its feathers that the bird takes the secretion of the oil gland in its beak and spreads it over its plumage. It is known that this gland, which opens on the rump, secretes a fatty substance of special composition, sometimes odorous, the exact role of which has not, up to the present, been exactly determined, but which seems to have the function of keeping the plumage supple and impermeable.

In the Herons and closely allied species there are zones on the skin where very thick patches of down develop; the bird takes in its beak this very friable down, the debris of which has the consistency of talcum powder, and with it covers its plumage; it also rubs its head and neck in it, and then, with the help of the claw of the median toe, which forms a sort of comb at the side, removes the powder when it is dry. It appears that this process removes the dirt which the bird gets while fishing, particularly the slime of fish.

The majority of birds bathe frequently, or more precisely, shake themselves in the water; the Swallows and Swifts plunge in for a brief moment in flight. Many species shuffle about in sand or dust as if to powder their plumage. The object of these various actions seems to be, in addition to cleaning the plumage, to counteract the irritation caused by parasites.

Common Heron sun-bathing.

A curious proceeding has occasionally been observed which has been given the name of "anting"; the bird seizes living ants in its beak and places them in its plumage, most often under the wings; or stretches itself out on an ants' nest. This action seems to give the bird great pleasure and seems also to help keep the plumage in good condition and to destroy parasites. Similar behaviour with regard to other objects such as lemons has also been observed, as well as the "smoke baths" of birds perched on chimneys.

Sun-bathing, which is most frequent in young birds, is also very difficult to explain; the bird stretches itself on the ground in a characteristic attitude with the tail and wings spread out; and even nocturnal birds have been seen performing the same actions.

Reaction in the face of danger varies according to the species and circumstances. Often the bird flies away or takes shelter in a place where the predator cannot follow it; many water birds dive. Certain aggressive species face the predator, attack it, and put it to flight; this behaviour is common among gregarious birds, even small ones (Swallows). Birds of prey in particular are mobbed by other species during the nesting season; it seems that hereditary enmities exist between certain birds and these are difficult to explain since the attacker is not the usual victim of the predator, such as a Buzzard being mobbed by Crows, Owls by many passerine

Unlike the Heron which faces the sun, this young Song-Thrush sun-bathes spread out on the ground. Other birds sun-bathe by perching with feathers fluffed out, neck stretched and beak open.

Teal preening.

birds, etc. Often the object of the attack is content to dodge the blows without reprisal, or even to fly away to get rid of its persecutors.

In many cases a bird's reaction to danger is to remain absolutely motionless. Often its coloration enables it to merge into the back-

Bittern on nest, preening. The oil gland is squeezed by the beak to extract the oil secretion in which the bird rubs its head and neck, then the rest of the plumage is smeared with oil by the beak.

ground, but even though this camouflage, which seems perfect to us, may not always deceive the predator, it is certain that immobility considerably reduces the chances of being discovered. The animal often flattens itself on the ground or on the contrary in cer-

tain cases it stretches up, and it is well known how easily a Bittern, for example, is indistinguishable from the surrounding reeds when it holds its neck up vertically. Occasionally birds have been seen "shamming dead" in a sort of cataleptic state; they have even

been known to die of fright, but this is very exceptional.

Reactions to danger are generally innate, at least in part. Young birds often react to any new large and moving object, but experiments have shown that certain characteristics of the object influence the reactions; thus a diagrammatic model of a bird of prey showing two spread wings, a short head and long tail, arouses fear in young goslings if it is moved in the normal direction, but if it is moved backwards they remain indifferent as then it has a slight resemblance to a Goose in flight. These innate reactions are, however, quickly corrected by the bird, which learns to know

real dangers, often with great precision; the majority of small birds react violently at the approach of a Goshawk or a European Sparrow-Hawk but the passing of a raptor which they need not fear such as Buzzard, Kite, Kestrel [Sparrow Hawk] leaves them indifferent. The cries of alarm they make are usually understood by several species and release self-preservation reactions in all those which hear them.

Sometimes, especially in certain social Corvidae, there is no innate knowledge, but the young react to the cries of alarm of the adults, and very rapidly associate them with the causes of danger; this is true education, an uncon-

Black-tailed Godwits preening.

scious oral transmission of acquired knowledge.

It is well known how often certain mammals, particularly the youngsters, indulge in play. There are far fewer examples among birds, but there are some very distinct cases. Young Kestrels [Sparrow Hawks], for example, have been observed playing like kittens with inanimate objects; some raptors occasionally pursue

50

their prey without trying to catch it, solely, it would seem, for the pleasure of the chase. Eider-Ducks let themselves be carried down by a torrent and then go up again and repeat the performance several times in succession. Aerial play is quite frequent; Crows or Jackdaws are often seen plunging one after the other into an ascending air current, to let themselves be carried up and then descend to repeat the cycle.

Certain demonstrations, like the mock combats of Grouse, imitations of those in spring, which are seen at the time of the partial return of sexual activity in autumn, could possibly be interpreted as play. But even when this appears to have no biological necessity, it is difficult to say whether it is really play, with all its psychological implications, or simply an exuberance of energy.

Black-tailed Godwit stretching itself.

A pair of Glossy Ibises.

Chapter II
REPRODUCTION

The annual cycle

As there are clearly defined seasons in the temperate regions of the northern hemisphere it is evident that the diverse activities of animals must be divided into periods forming an annual rhythm. But in tropical regions also where conditions of life appear to be much more uniform, and the breeding season of birds may occur at almost any time of the year, it has been established that, in the great majority of cases, each species taken individually has a distinct periodicity.

One is led to believe that the action of the various factors which govern the sequence of activities of an animal is much less than it appears, and actually, in spite of numerous experimental studies and field observations, the precise cause of the annual cycle of birds is still unknown.

Very diagrammatically the annual cycle of a bird may be summed up as follows:

Arrival of the male in the nesting area—Song and establishment of an individual territory —Formation of the pair—Nest building—Laying of eggs, incubation and rearing of young— Departure from the nesting area.

In addition there are the moults occurring at varying seasons once or twice a year and also in some cases a temporary renewal, more or less distinct, of sexual activity after the autumn moult but usually reduced to song and establishment of a territory.

Variations of detail in the general scheme are innumerable. The changes of habitat range from simple local movements to long migrations; the pair may be formed before return to the nesting area; the nest may be partly built by the male before the arrival of the female; there may be one clutch or several, etc. At all events there is always a distinct rhythm and its different phases are closely connected; moreover, it must not be forgotten that the divisions which it is necessary to make in order to examine each one in detail are profoundly artificial. As a result, any generalisations which can be made are always somewhat arbitrary.

It should be noted that in the constitution of this cycle each one of the acts is controlled by a final objective which is more or less distant and has no part in the conditions of the moment. Thus a bird will leave an easy existence in a region with a mild and equable climate to undertake a long journey in order to arrive just at the right time to nest during the few weeks of arctic summer. Likewise large birds of prey lay and incubate in mountains before the end of winter under climatic conditions which may seem particularly unfavourable, so that the young, whose growth is slow, may benefit from the abundant food in spring and be able to fend for themselves before the following winter.

It has been established that the developmental cycle is determined in such a way that its most critical phase occurs at the most favourable period, and it seems that, at all events, a maximum supply of food at the time of the rearing of the young is the determining factor.

Thus in a tropical region with alternating dry and wet seasons insectivorous birds nest at the beginning of the rainy season when insects emerge, while the fruit and seed-eaters do not nest until towards its end, when their food is ripening. Birds of prey wait for the dry season when their

Attitudes in display of Grouse: a), b) ▶
Sage-cock; c) *Dusky Grouse calling;*
d), e) *Black Grouse.*

prey is most abundant. On the islands in the Mediterranean, Eleonora's Falcon does not lay its eggs until the latter part of July and feeds its young on the plentiful food supply provided by the southward post-breeding migration of European summer visitors.

Birds which are actuated by a rigid instinct so far as reproduction and migration are concerned have no consciousness of the final object of their actions; the question then arises as to what are the immediate determining causes—for example how present conditions affect the development of instinctive reactions the useful consequences of which are remote; and how the seasonal cycle of the bird is linked to the environment.

The Ptarmigan assumes its summer plumage by a gradual moult which is correlated with the disappearance of the patches of snow in the mountains in spring. In autumn it assumes a grey plumage differing from the brown summer dress, so that this bird has three moults a year.

Beginning of courtship display by the Waved Albatross. In the foreground is a Galapagos Mocking-bird.

Wandering Albatrosses (Kerguelen Islands). The male has extended his wings (span: 10 ft.) in front of the female who is about to adopt the same posture. The two birds then approach each other until their beaks touch.

Tree-creepers roost in a crack in the trunk of a tree, or, as shown in the illustration, in a small hole which they excavate in soft bark. With feathers fluffed out, clinging on by the feet and supported by the tail, the bird can well withstand the cold of a long winter night even if partly covered by snow.

Numerous studies have proved that the sexual behaviour of birds is directly controlled, both from a psychological and physiological point of view, by endocrine secretions. Even a very brief summary of the results obtained would be far too extensive, and we will simply mention that the male is controlled only by the action of the male hormone, while the female is dominated by both male and female hormones which are secreted simultaneously in the ovary. Each of these two secretions acts on definite elements determining behaviour, but their

distribution varies according to the species.

It is the seasonal variation in the activity of the gonads, an activity which is itself dependent on the pituitary, which controls the annual cycle of a bird.

It should be noted that the partial resumption in autumn of sexual activity, due to renewed activity of the gonads, causes a temporary appearance of masculine characteristics in certain females, as a result of a relatively larger proportion of male hormones, such as for instance the yellow beak in certain races of

Growth of a young Great Potoo. Trinidad. The chick grows up on the spot where the egg has been laid. With the loss of its nestling down it progressively assumes the posture of the adult in which the bird resembles the branch of a tree.

Starlings, the song and territorial instinct in Robins, etc.

These facts have led to investigations on the action of various seasonal factors on endocrine activity, in particular the effect of light as, in temperate regions, its annual variations are considerable.

It has been shown that light acts directly on the pituitary and that an artificial increase in the length of daylight accelerates the maturing of the gonads. In the same way decrease of daylight leads to a regression of organs which have already developed. These facts

were evidently known to Japanese and Dutch bird-fanciers, who have long used artificial light, or kept their captives in darkness, in order to make them sing out of season.

Variations of temperature and quantity of food have no effect; in certain species it seems that the variations of muscular activity resulting from the differences in the length of daylight may have a special influence. In equatorial regions where the length of daylight is practically constant, it seems that differences in humidity may play a predominant part, but our knowledge of this subject is extremely vague because of the large number of particular cases.

Whatever the factor concerned may be, it is important to note that the same conditions may act differently, not only on different species, but also on different populations of the same species. Thus, in winter, the populations of birds in temperate regions may be composed of residents and also other individuals which have come from distant places with a harder climate. The approach of spring leads members of the former group to scatter over their breeding territory and stimulates

Nightingale on nest.

the others to make their return journey. Conversely the diverse populations of a species with a wide distribution are influenced, according to the regions, by varying factors which nevertheless lead to the same final results.

External factors, therefore, do not seem to be the only cause in determining physiological variations; it seems that they intervene only to regularise an internal rhythm which has its independent existence. The degree to which they act seems to vary according to species and their action is perhaps only necessary at determined moments.

Although the real existence of this internal rhythm may be questionable, numerous special cases seem to confirm it. Thus the Sooty Tern breeds every nine months in Ascension Island where there is an equable climate and abundant food. In Australia, Puffins observed over many years lay, to within about three days, on the same date every year, certain females having laid for years in succession on precisely the same date. Elsewhere birds nest at a fixed date even if the

rainy season varies by several weeks. Removing birds from one hemisphere to another produces varying, but characteristic, results. Though certain species quickly adapt themselves to new conditions, others seem thrown out of gear and no longer nest at the usual time and some keep to their primitive rhythm, differing by six months from that of the birds of the new country in which they have been made to live. Even their descendants may keep to the ancestral rhythm, which is not adapted to the new conditions until after several generations.

The effect of external conditions is evidenced in the case of birds of semi-desert regions where breeding takes place during a very short rainy season which does

not even occur every year. They get ready for nesting well before the rains, but their gonads regress if rain does not come. Elsewhere chance circumstances, for example the sudden appearance, following a flood, of materials necessary for constructing a nest, have caused birds to breed at an unusual time.

In spite of the arguments which the above facts bring forward it must be admitted that reproduction and migration are dependent on psychological and physiological conditions varying according to species, but acting on each other with such subtlety that the reality of an internal physiological rhythm has not been established with certainty in all cases, despite the numerous arguments put forward in favour of it.

Song and territory

If the sounds uttered by various species are examined it will soon be seen that it is difficult to define with any precision what is meant by the "song" of a bird. There is no criterion for fixing where the song begins and the calls end.

It is evident that the aesthetic or sentimental emotion which they can produce in us does not come into the question, any more than the complexity of the melody. If the song of the Nightingale is a song in every meaning of the word, what can be said of that of the Fantail Warbler, that minute Warbler of the marshes of the Mediterranean, which is content with regular repetition of a sharp little note, very poor if compared to the call-note of the Wood-Lark? The conditions under which it is uttered, however, leave no doubt as to its nature. Still the varying circumstances under which birds sing, the effects of this song, which sometimes seems to be uttered solely for pleasure, are too diverse to form a basis for a precise definition. As often happens when occupied with biological as well as systematic questions concerning birds, one is confronted with a homogeneous col-

Robin bringing food to the nest.

Female Crossbill on nest preparing to receive the courtship offering of food from the male. The movements of the female are exactly like those of a young bird begging for food.

lection of facts so varied in their details that it is impossible to find a simple formula for them. It is often only by a general examination and by many comparisons that it is possible to classify certain particular examples.

In most cases the song is distinguished from other vocal manifestations of the bird by its frequent repetition, often by its power, and also by a certain complexity of melody. The circumstances in which it is uttered are always more or less correlated with the reproductive cycle.

The calls are simpler, more varied in individual species and are correlated with relatively well defined situations. It is quite easy to distinguish the call-notes, some of which are particular to migratory flights, frequently uttered in flight to maintain cohesion in scattered flocks, the call of the

mother bird conducting her chicks, the alarm notes which are understood by several species, etc. Other calls which may be restricted to the breeding season, but differ from the song, have not always a very clear significance. Birds even incorporate some of their calls in their song.

An almost constant feature of the song, which also applies to the calls, is its specificity; except in very rare examples of fortuitous resemblances which are probably not apparent to the bird, and of more or less perfect imitations, a species can be identified with certainty by its song alone.

It is now generally accepted that, in spite of numerous attempts at musical notation, an exact transcription of songs and calls is practically impossible. Onomatopoeic representations, often used for want of something better,

can at best be only very approximate, but in all languages they are quite frequently the origin of names given to birds. For instance, the words *cuculus*, the Cuckoo, and *upupa*, the Hoopoe, have served as arguments in favour of the pronunciation of the Latin *u* as *oo*.

The enormous advances in the quality of recording equipment over the past few years have enabled us to extend at a rapid rate our knowledge of vocal sounds. Sonograms—graphics which give a time-scale of the intensity and pitch of sounds emitted—make precise study possible. They have shown, among other things, that a bird is capable of producing simultaneously two independent sounds bearing no harmonic relation one with the other. It has also been established that the notes can succeed one another to an extremely rapid cadence—so rapid, in fact, that the human ear cannot separate them. Where we hear only a single note the bird must perceive a melody.

Recordings have also enabled us to research the reactions of birds to their song and calls and to carry out experiments on how birds learn to sing.

Nor should it be forgotten that recordings are now widely available which provide remarkable documentation on bird-song the whole world over; indeed this subject is so fully documented that any attempt at description here would be futile. We shall merely mention, as a reminder, apart from the well-known and very familiar bird-songs, those of the waders whose purity of tone often greatly compensates for the simplicity of melody; and those of the small aquatic birds, Rails, Moorhens [Gallinules], certain Warblers, etc., all of which have raucous, somewhat croaking notes of great power. The song of the Grasshopper Warbler and its near relatives is hardly distinguishable from the trill of a grasshopper and that of the European Nightjar is a continuous churring mixed with clapping of the wings. Certain Owls utter notes of regular cadence at long intervals.

In exotic birds the variety is even greater and the peculiar notes uttered by some species have earned them such names as Forge-Bird, Bell-Bird, Trumpeter, etc.

Finally there are cases where the song is replaced by non-vocal sounds, the most classic being that of certain Woodpeckers which produce a drumming noise by striking the beak against a branch. Several species of Snipe produce a bleating sound by the vibration of the fanned-out tail feathers during a special flight; the Stork, which is voiceless, has substituted a sound like castanets, produced by clapping its beak.

Among closely allied species there are quite often resemblances which enable the characteristics of a group to be defined (Buntings and Pipits, for example). In

Left, Grasshopper Warbler; right, flight-song of Pipit.

some cases, on the other hand, the differences are so great that two species of similar appearance have very different songs (Chiff-chaff and Willow-Warbler).

Various populations of the same species, identical in other respects, may show local differences in song which are sometimes quite considerable.

The song, stimulated by the male hormone, is chiefly uttered during the breeding season, particularly at the beginning, but not by any means does every bird have this tendency to the same degree, and the same species may show differences in different regions. There are some, such as the Wren and Cetti's Warbler, which sing throughout almost the whole year, hardly stopping during the moult. Others like the Chaffinch have periods of frequent song, lasting several months but starting and ending suddenly; finally certain species sing spasmodically (e.g. Hawfinch).

Many songs are more or less resumed after the autumn moult, but are less frequent and often less pure than in spring, though in certain individuals they may be prolonged throughout the winter, except during extreme cold. The Pigmy Owl is peculiar in having an autumn song which is quite different from its spring song.

During the breeding season the song is generally very frequent but unevenly distributed according to the circumstances. Thus the Redstart sings when he is establishing his territory, sings again when the female arrives and most of all when he shows her the nest-site, but stops while she is building; he resumes his song to some extent during the laying of the eggs, much more during their incubation, but stops when they hatch and does not sing again unless there is a second clutch. The Nightingale sings without ceasing from the time of its arrival until the hatching of the eggs. Many small passerine birds stop, or only sing very occasionally, after the pair has been formed; some even start to sing during migration, others continue during the rearing of the young and the European Robin, which stops at this period, starts again when the young are independent.

Some birds sing all day long and even during the night (Nightingale, Reed-Warbler, Sedge-Warbler, etc.); others sing at certain hours, principally in the morning and at the end of the day, and others only sing at times of great excitement.

Atmospheric conditions also play their part; song which is at its maximum during fine weather often is not stopped because of warm rain but wind, drought or great cold may cause it to cease temporarily.

Uttered under varying conditions and influenced by very diverse factors, song plays an important part in the life of a bird which is difficult to define in all circumstances. It seems that

Intimidation postures:
left, Robin;
right, Common Tern.

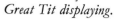

Great Tit displaying.

descent, the Fantail Warbler ascends and descends as if it were hung on a piece of elastic, and utters its call at each oscillation. In tropical America, the Jacarini, a little black Finch, rises vertically for a yard, turns a somersault in the air, calling "bzt", and lets itself fall again. Though certain songs are almost always uttered in flight, there are others which are restricted to periods of particular sexual activity and to display flights (Serin, Greenfinch, etc.).

When the pair is formed the song continues to keep possible rivals at a distance, but just like the attitudes of display, which it often accompanies, and from which it can hardly be separated, it strengthens the unity of the pair. It could be said, if human similes were allowed, that this show of virility in the male commands the respect of his rivals and arouses the admiration of his companion. Song also intervenes in many circumstances in the life of the pair; thus it is by this means that the male Redstart and the Pied Flycatcher indicate the nest-site to the female.

Few females sing. In the European Robin the song forms part

this expenditure of energy—externalisation of a certain state of well-being—of which, however, the bird is unconscious—might be quite superfluous at certain moments, in the same way, for example, as the existence of certain ornamental feathers which are not used except for display. But like these feathers the effect produced may be of the greatest importance to the bird, and this is especially the case in the most frequent type of song, that which is associated with the possession of territory. The song asserts the presence and identity of the bird and its repetition at the same

places attests the occupation of the territory. This will then be a warning to other males, a defence against intrusion, and for the unpaired females it indicates the existence of a possible mate.

The effect of song may be increased by the conditions under which it is uttered. Though some birds, such as the Nightingale, sing when hidden, many perch in exposed positions. Others, as if to make more impression, sing in flight such as the Skylark and Wood-Lark for instance, which sing continuously above their territory. Pipits fly up vertically and sing during their planing of a number of temporary masculine characteristics. In some species the female sings in special circumstances such as when a strange male enters the territory. There are sometimes duets between two mates which seem very significant of the union of the pair. The two songs may follow each other in such a way that they seem like a single song (Guianan Partridge, Gonolek).

As a general rule there is an innate tendency in birds to sing the characteristic song of the species, but this tendency is very unevenly developed. Some birds, even if they are artificially isolated from birth, will sing the normal song without learning it; others, under the same conditions, will have a different song, generally a more or less varied twittering with little differentiation. They have to hear the song of their species to be able to sing themselves. There are intermediate cases where the song only needs to be perfected. It is not always the more complicated songs which have to be learnt; the melody of the Blackcap can be almost perfect without being learnt.

It seems that often the song of the adult, heard during the first weeks of existence, "imprints" the young bird which sings it without hesitation the following spring. Nevertheless it is known that in the Chaffinch it is only the songs of the adult males uttered at the end of the winter which enable the males born the preceding year to execute their nor-mal song. It seems that if the young birds do not hear it at this period they can never learn it and instead utter a sort of uniform trill all their lives. It would be interesting to know if this abnormal song produces the same effect as the normal song in the life of the bird.

Birds isolated at birth are able to learn the songs of those with which they are brought in contact, but sometimes abandon these to assume their own song if they hear it. It is well known that bird-fanciers take advantage of this fact by teaching their birds different airs by means of musical instruments. On the other hand, under natural conditions, some birds may "imitate" the songs of other species. Fragments of various songs or calls may be interpolated from time to time in a very characteristic song (Sedge-Warbler, Icterine Warbler); it is probable, moreover, that there are often fortuitous resemblances, but there are species whose normal song is nothing but a mixture of various sounds. The most typical from this point of view among European birds is probably the Marsh-Warbler which in a few moments may include calls or fragments of song of Greenfinches, Goldfinches, Sparrows, Tits, Swallows, Whitethroats, Partridges and many others, occasionally interspersed with its own notes. Some imitations are excellent, others less so, and it is not known how the bird learns them.

Other imitations are of a diff-erent character. Jays and Starlings, for example, add quite good imitations of various calls and noises to their normal repertoire. The significance of these imitations is not clear; it is perhaps a sort of game. Though quite rare in the wild, imitations are more frequent in captive birds and there is no need to dwell on those of Parrots and a number of other species.

It is a common observation that in spring the majority of males sing at the same places, on the same perches, just before the building of the nest. It is curious that this fact was known for a long time before its significance was apparent to zoologists. Although various allusions were made to it by older authors, it is only about fifty years since it was recognised that the establishment of a well-defined territory had considerable importance in the life of many birds.

At the end of the winter flocks of little Finches, Buntings, Chaffinches or others are frequently seen in the fields; they search for food together and fly off together to feed elsewhere or to shelter in a bush. But one day a male bird is seen to separate from the flock and perch conspicuously on the branch of a leafless tree. He stays there for some time and then returns to the flock where he is lost to sight. As the days pass, and especially when the weather is fine, his visits become more frequent. He chooses various points and starts

to sing from one or the other. Before long he no longer returns to the flock which gradually disperses. To begin with he still tolerates his old companions near him, then rapidly all intruders are chased off. If another birds sings nearby his song is intensified, the neighbour replies and a veritable vocal contest ensues. The bird is definitely established in his "territory"; he has fixed its boundaries and his song announces this far and wide. Sooner or later a female joins him and the nest is built there.

This sort of behaviour is very widespread. The migrants may not go through so many stages and their territory may be chosen very quickly after their arrival, but the principle always remains the same.

The establishment of the territory is almost always the prerogative of the male, except when the roles of the sexes are reversed such as in the Phalaropes. Sometimes the territory is not established till after the formation of the pair. Usually the female is less attached to it than her mate, her knowledge of its boundaries is poor and she may even build a nest outside it, and the male is then obliged to conquer a part of a neighbouring territory.

Often all the activities of reproduction take place within the territory; this is the case in many small passerine birds. The territory varies greatly in extent, ranging from $\frac{1}{4}$ to $2\frac{1}{2}$ acres for smaller species to over 60 square miles for large birds of prey such as the Golden Eagle. Moreover, it may be divided into several independent sections. The same pair may therefore have one territory for nesting, another for feeding, sometimes some distance from the first, and even a third, a temporary one, for pairing (Greenshank) and all three are

Bearded Tit, male and female (the latter carrying a dragon-fly). In this species the birds pair off at a very early age, which is exceptional among the Passerines.

defended against all intruders, but the feeding territory not being so well defined is defended less than the others.

Defence of territory is chiefly made by song which is intensified as any intruder approaches. Often the intruder goes away without persisting, especially if it is a bird inhabiting the neighbourhood, as each individual is quick to learn the boundaries of its neighbours. But when a newcomer persists, for instance if a bird with no territory seeks to establish itself, menacing attitudes are added to the song. The attitudes of these aggressive displays are peculiar to each species; the Blue-headed Wagtail stands erect, head thrown back and the chest feathers fluffed out; the Common Tern stretches out its neck with the beak pointing towards the ground, wings hanging down and tail raised. The next stage is pursuit in which the female may take part. Very rarely there is a real fight, but the dispute, interposed with periods of rest, may last several hours.

It is very unusual for the owner to be dispossessed, but it sometimes has to give up a part of its domain, particularly in a thickly populated area where there is no longer any free ground. In this event the installation of the last arrivals is not done by a progressive narrowing of the existing territories; the most aggressive males, which perhaps already possess the largest areas, retain their positions and the newcomers are interspersed among the others.

The intensity of defence of a territory is variable. Species which are less belligerent than others react more calmly, being content to guard it by song. Some are so aggressive that they attack birds of other species which pass near-by, even if they are not birds of prey, and several birds may unite against these latter.

Defence may be weak at the beginning of the season and intensify after the arrival of the female. On the contrary in other species defence may diminish on the arrival of the female, and likewise during the incubation of the eggs and rearing of the young.

When the owner of a territory disappears it is usually very quickly replaced.

Territorial instinct takes many very diverse forms, but whatever

Common Heron. Intimidation display.

Pair of Pink-footed Geese. Geese are among the few birds that mate for life.

they may be, everything occurs as if on its own territory the bird has a sense of superiority. This superiority by its very nature changes when a bird enters any neighbouring territory. Such trespassing is done furtively and if surprised the intruder retreats. The difference in the psychological state, as well as the role of the song, is shown by the case of the Robin kept in a cage near to territories occupied by other Robins. The captive bird sang at the approach of his relatives which retreated without coming close to the cage; in fact he defended a territory which he could not enter, but which his neighbours also could not enter, though for quite a different reason.

Various interpretations of the origin of territorial instinct have

been advanced. The practical advantages are obvious, a good knowledge of the domain enabling the bird to exploit it to the full (food, shelter, etc.). However, it seems that the most general advantage brought by the territory is in the regularisation of the relations between individuals at a critical period of their existence by considerably diminishing the risks of upsetting the reproductive activities. The establishment of this territory more or less reserved for specific activities, more or less large, more or less temporary, more or less well-defended, appears to be the crystallisation of the conflict between gregarious and individualistic tendencies, shown simultaneously but in extremely variable proportions.

The pronounced intolerance—particularly in the male—during the period of sexual excitement leads the bird to isolate itself in a domain which in some way is an external projection of its individuality, the expression of its superiority over other things. By a sort of ritualisation of relations among the individuals of which there are many other examples elsewhere, a minimum of useless expenditure of energy and of combats which may become disastrous is achieved. This is of advantage to the individual as well as to the species.

When the behaviour of a species is studied it is almost always found to be a reflection of its social tendencies. Some birds, in particular many Passerines, will not tolerate the presence of other individuals of the same species at any time during the breeding season, others show more gregarious tendencies by grouping their territories into little colonies, even though large areas of apparently suitable habitat may remain uninhabited (Blue-headed Wagtail). Linnets group their territories in the same way, but these are confined to nesting activities, the search for food being carried on elsewhere without competition.

In certain Ducks a temporary territory is established solely for display. Gregarious birds like Rooks and Jackdaws defend a common territory round their colony. Many sea-birds which search for their food in unlimited space nest in colonies. The nests are almost adjoining and each pair only defends its own nest and the small space around it; but in such cases it is hardly possible to call it territory.

The gregarious tendencies of birds with territory may be shown in an unexpected manner such as in the male Fork-tailed Flycatcher which is particularly aggressive and attacks every bird which passes near its nest, but leaves its territory at night to join other males in a communal roost. When the population of an area is dense Dartford Warblers, which usually have a normal territorial behaviour, group together in several pairs to defend a common territory. Finally in very few species, for example the Oystercatcher, the territorial instinct does not seem to exist clearly.

Among Gannets as among other sea-birds which nest in colonies, the territorial instinct only manifests itself at the immediate approaches to the nest.

69

Display of Common Heron preceding coition.

The formation of the pair

The great majority of birds are monogamous but temporary pairing is the most usual, and the union does not last longer than one breeding season, or even a single brood if there are several in a season.

Some species, however, remain paired for several years, or even —which is very exceptional in animals—for life, such as certain Corvidae and some birds of prey (especially Owls), Swans, Geese, some Woodpeckers, Penguins, etc. Storks separate during the winter but re-unite again every year at the nest which is probably the link which keeps them together. This must also be the case in Shearwaters and Storm Petrels which have a tendency to form permanent pairs, as well as the Albatrosses which, despite their solitary wanderings, return to each other from one year to another. It has been established that in the Royal Albatross, birds have remained paired for 10 years.

These lasting unions are sometimes preceded by a period of "betrothal" which may be quite lengthy. Young Jackdaws and Geese form pairs in the spring following their birth and although they do not nest till the following year when they have attained sexual maturity, yet remain together during the intervening period. In the Bearded Tit, one of the very few species of small Passerines known to pair for life, the union is made very early between young birds, less than two months after their birth, and before they have assumed adult plumage which, especially in the males, differs greatly from that of the juvenile.

In permanent pairs if one of the couple dies it is soon replaced, but in the case of Geese the survivor often remains single.

Accidental bigamy occurs from time to time in many species, usually when a male which is already paired takes up with a neighbouring female whose mate has died. This tendency is more prevalent when the males take little part in the rearing of the young (Wren); there may also be successive polygamy, the male having one mate at a time, who is abandoned for another as soon as she has laid (Pied Flycatcher).

Storks displaying on their nest.

Polygamy is general in some species such as certain gallinaceous birds, Rheas, etc.; in the latter the male alone broods the eggs, which are laid in a common nest. In Central America Wagler's Oropendola establishes colonies where only the females build the nests and the males successively court several females as soon as their nest is completed and take no part in bringing up the young. In the Bishop Birds it is the male which successively builds several nests to which he conducts a female each time.

Polyandry is found only when the roles of the sexes are partly reversed as in the Painted Snipe, Tinamous, etc. Finally there are species where the sexes live separately and do not meet except for copulation such as certain Grouse, Bustards, Birds of Paradise, Ruffs, etc.

The formation of pairs is one of the most interesting aspects of bird behaviour and the theoretical importance from the point of view of evolution is considerable.

Unfortunately observation of this in the wild is extremely difficult and there are few reliable data except for a very small number of species.

Close observations have been made principally when the male establishes a territory before the arrival of the female. A male Blue-headed Wagtail, singing one April morning perched on the handle of a plough, suddenly sees a female arrive, approach him and settle in a nearby field; they call to each other and then he leaves his perch, goes close to her, chest puffed out, wings hanging down and circles round her, though she does not move and appears indifferent. He returns to his perch and sings while she disappears in the vegetation. Practically nothing has happened, but the link has been formed because an hour later a neighbouring male, which up to then had been tolerated, is fiercely chased away when he approaches and the female will not go away again.

The female European Robin is not accepted so quickly; when she appears before the male, he sings and assumes an aggressive attitude, but does not chase her away as he would another male; on the contrary he retreats when she approaches and she often sings a little. This stratagem may last some time with interruptions while both birds go away to feed. Usually everything is finished at the end of some hours; the female is accepted and does not leave her new territory.

When the two sexes have different plumage like the Blue-headed Wagtail, the male seems to recognise the female at once by her coloration. In the Robin the sexes are alike, but an experienced observer—and furthermore the birds themselves—can distinguish them by small differences of bearing and gait. In spite of this, the aggressive tendencies of the male show that his territorial instinct is not immediately suppressed when faced by his future companion.

This conflict between two opposing tendencies is much more

Display of Ducks: left, Pintail; right, Red-breasted Merganser.

marked in some species and quite a ceremonial is developed so that the female, who hesitates to approach in the face of the hostile manifestations of the male, may be accepted without difficulty (Common Heron, Night Heron, etc.). The hostile tendency may even never be entirely suppressed and gestures of recognition are employed throughout the breeding season. In the Common Heron there is the erection of the long tapering plumes with frequent offering of a twig when the two birds meet on the nest.

In some species which remain a long time in flocks, pairs may be formed before dispersal, but it is very difficult to know what occurs. In Magpies and Jays, pairing may take place during a kind of confabulation, at which sometimes a large number of birds gather together and the significance of which is not clear. Ducks have collective ceremonies which begin very early in the season. The males parade round the females with movements varying according to the species, head raised then lowered horizontally, or thrown backwards touching the back, breast raised above the water, tail raised, etc. The scene often ends with the pursuit of a

female by several males, but other females may join the mêlée. It seems that during the course of these reunions the males and females get to know each other individually and that the females only consent to copulate with the partner they have chosen, and then go off with him.

What are the factors which determine the choice of mates? It is very difficult to decide. Though the chance of meeting must often play a large part, in species where immediate agreement seems to be the rule a female will visit several males before settling down, or a male

White Storks greeting each other with ritual display on arrival at the nest.

may be indifferent to several females before accepting one. Perhaps the birds are not in the necessary physiological condition. Perhaps it is a question of choice, but, if so, on what basis is it made? The classic hypothesis of Darwin that females choose the most ornamental males and those displaying their adornments to the best advantage does not always hold good in the face of facts. It may be plausible for birds which, like Ducks, pair when they are in flocks, or in those where the females betake themselves to the places where the males are displaying, such as Grouse, Ruffs, etc. In the latter case, moreover, it is hardly possible to speak of the formation of a pair since theirs is no lasting union. On the other hand, in solitary birds chance seems to play a large role in the joining of two partners and the spectacular displays, which are

usually rare in these species, are sexual displays which do not occur till later when the pair is united and the female sees hardly any other male but her own.

Formation of the pair may occur a long time before the building of the nest, for instance in the autumn in the Hazel Grouse, December in the Robin and February or March in many small resident passerine birds of Europe. In the migratory birds, and especially those which arrive late in the season, nest-building may begin as soon as the pair is formed. The period of "betrothal"

may be long, bad weather may temporarily cause the birds to separate but a day arrives when they begin to show the internal change which is taking place. They are seen from time to time carrying materials as if they were going to build a nest and then letting them drop; later new activities begin to appear. In April in a firwood two Crested Tits flit about among the trees exploring the branches in the usual manner of Tits but one of them suddenly repeatedly utters the call of a young bird. The other bird flies towards her carrying a beakful of food which she accepts, then they stay together for a moment facing each other, pivoting round with wings fluttering horizontally before renewing their quest for food.

This feeding of the female by the male is found in nearly all groups of birds. In the Cormorants, Herons and some others

Display of Amherst Pheasant.

74

*Little Terns. Female on nest being offered
a small fish by her mate.*

the action is slightly different; the two partners rub their beaks together, or one seizes the beak of the other. It is remarkable that in these species the gestures are exactly like those of a young bird begging for food from the adult. In the same way Pigeons make the movement of regurgitation of "milk".

In all this it is the gesture which counts and not the food for which the female seems to have no particular need; for instance in a pair of captive European Robins, the female begged for food while perched on the edge of a receptacle heaving with meal-worms. In the Gulls which disgorge food in front of the female, as they do before the chicks, all the gestures may be perfectly carried out, without any food being actually transmitted.

It is difficult to explain this transposition to infantile behaviour, but at all events it is certain that the ritual has great emotional value for the adults and its repetition reinforces the links which unite the pair. Later the female will often continue to be fed by the male, but though during incubation this feeding is of practical value, its value as a link between the two mates remains.

Its absence in the gallinaceous birds, which do not form lasting pairs, is significant. It has not been observed in the Wren, which has polygamous tendencies; on the other hand in birds which remain paired for several years it is not started till the building of the nest has begun.

The following stage is true courtship display in which the birds may show, by gesticulations or dances combined with songs or calls, one of the most extraordinary performances in the animal world. Varying with the species very specialised displays are made at various times during the breeding cycle, the most characteristic usually being shortly before and during the period of copulation, but they may even precede pairing as is the case in some Ducks; on other occasions they continue throughout the breeding season and some also serve as gestures of intimidation against rivals. Many of them, and not the least spectacular, have only been observed in captive birds, and their significance cannot be specified.

The movements of the display may be executed by the male

Dalmatian Pelicans displaying on nest before mating.

alone in front of the female, who appears indifferent, but whose emotion is shown by small movements apparently insignificant but nevertheless characteristic, often for instance by little taps with the beak on the ground as if to pick up food.

76

Each year the Ruffs return in spring to the same piece of ground for their social ceremonies. The males have then grown their ruffs which differ in colour in each individual. They challenge each other without defending any particular territory (upper photograph where the bird on the right is in the threat attitude). When a Reeve appears the males crouch before her, their ruffs fully expanded and their beaks pointed towards the ground (lower photograph). She makes her choice and solicits the chosen male by caressing the feathers of his ruff with her beak.

Display of male Black Grouse.

77

The Peacock has the most classic display of this type, which it is unnecessary to describe. Many Pheasants also display beside the female, bending towards her to show off the greatest possible extent of their ornamental feathers. The ruffs of the Golden and Amherst Pheasants are spread like a lateral fan and hide almost the whole head, leaving only the crest and eye uncovered; the eye alternately opens and shuts, revealing the pale yellow iris. The Monal Pheasant, in addition to the lateral display, makes a movement whereby he first shows his front, then quickly turns round so that the entire surface of his metallic plumage shines in a multicoloured flash.

The Great Argus Pheasant bends towards the female and moves round her in narrowing circles, then suddenly spreads his enormous wings in front of her. He brings them forward over his head forming an enormous circular screen spangled with ocelli and surmounted by the two tail feathers, which fill her field of vision. This display takes place in clearings in the Malayan forest which are the property of the males and used from one generation to another.

Many Pheasants have blue or red caruncles which become swollen during the breeding season and may assume enormous proportions during the display; thus the head of the Bulwer Pheasant disappears between two huge narrow blue facial lobes from which only the beak emerges.

Though Grouse are less ornamented than the majority of Pheasants, they have no less extraordinary displays; the attitude in all is very much the same, neck rigid and swollen, wings hanging down, tail raised and spread, but the details of their ornamentations vary remarkably. Some American species in particular have pouches of naked coloured skin, normally hidden by the feathers, but which are expanded during display; such as the red swellings of the Dusky Grouse, the yellow swellings of the Prairie Chicken, which when expanded raise the tufts of elongated plumes making the bird look as if it had long ears, and the enormous pectoral pouch of the Sage Grouse. All these pouches act as sound boxes for the ventriloquial calls which can be heard from a great distance. In addition to the whistles, coos, and the most varied noises they utter, some Grouse produce yet other sounds; for instance the Ruffed Grouse by vibrating its wings makes a noise like a tambourine, and the rubbing of the wings of the Sage Grouse on the stiff feathers of the neck produces the sound of rustling silk.

Sacs of skin swollen out with air are not peculiar to the Grouse, but are also found in a number of other species. The Frigate Birds have an enormous red sac which swells out under the neck, certain Bustards also have a pectoral sac and that of the Australian Bustard, which is covered with feathers, stretches to the ground like a cascade of down. The Umbrella

Umbrella Bird displaying.

Birds, those Cotingas with peculiar ornamentations, also have a pouch which swells, but varies in appearance according to the local races, as a result of the great variability of the feathers which cover it.

Though our knowledge of this subject is still very incomplete it would be easy to quote many other examples of remarkable displays, such as the dances of the Cock-of-the-Rock, Manakins, etc., but certainly special mention should be made of the Birds of Paradise. Actually there is no other group of birds with such a variety of ornaments and such singular movements in display.

The classic Great Bird of Paradise—whose plumes were in such great demand for millinery as to arouse concern for the extinction of the species—begins by uttering loud and raucous calls. It then starts to dance on its branch. head lowered and gently swinging from right to left; the oscillations increase, the wings open, quivering, the long plumes of the

flanks are lifted, then suddenly the bird bends forward, lowers the wings and erects the two big waving sprays of plumes. It remains in this position for one or two minutes and then suddenly resumes its normal position as if nothing had happened.

Allied species have similar behaviour but with some variations; the Emperor William's Bird of Paradise and the Prince Rudolph's Bird of Paradise, for example, hang head down, spreading their billowing feathers around them.

The ornamentations of other species—plaques with metallic reflections, fans of black feathers looking like velvet or watered silk, specialised feathers of all sorts—are moved and distorted to give the bird an abnormal appearance. The Magnificent Bird of Paradise presents himself to the female in the form of a rectangle of green velvet glittering with a series of little blue bars, the beak only projecting and behind it a halo of pale yellow. In the Twelve-wired Bird of Paradise the head is surrounded by an enormous dark disk edged with brilliant green and the twelve long thread-like plumes are bent forwards; from time to time he opens his beak to show the green interior. This gaping, showing a coloured palate, is quite common among Birds of Paradise and apple green is the usual colour, as in the King Bird of Paradise, Magnificent Bird of Paradise, etc.; but white and yellow also occur.

The Bower-Birds, related to the true Birds of Paradise, do not possess such queer adornments, but are distinguished by a very special type of display. The males construct a kind of passage or tunnel of twigs in front of which on a platform they place various objects, such as little bones, shells, flowers, fruits, feathers, usually of a particular colour, varying according to the species. Sometimes the interior of the tunnel is smeared with the same colour, made of a mixture of saliva, mashed up grass, fruit pulp, etc. The male keeps the bower in order, replaces faded

Above, beginning of the display of the Great Bird of Paradise. It swings from right to left with the long flank plumes raised behind the wings; in the climax of the display it bends forward and these plumes are fully erected like a spray.
Below, Rifle-bird displaying. The broad wings spread wide open make this Bird of Paradise look like a huge black butterfly. Every few seconds the wings are brought together and then spread out again; the head which was inclined to one side is suddenly bent towards the other side and the gorget of shining feathers flashes a metallic green.

flowers and fruits that have withered and when a female arrives she installs herself in it to watch the display. During this the male often presents her with one of the objects he has accumulated, and both may remain for a long time completely motionless.

Not much is known of the details of these manifestations and their interpretation is difficult; it has been suggested that the construction of a "bower" is not entirely governed by a sexual stimulus, but is a kind of play which might even be described as "pre-aesthetic".

One could describe many other types of displays but we will conclude by mentioning the Lyre-Bird, another inhabitant of this oceanic region so rich in singular creatures. This bird sings, erects his tail of varied feathers, and then at the height of excitement turns his tail over in front, showing the underside whilst he himself is entirely hidden.

Displays as spectacular as this are by no means the general rule among birds, but if those of our familiar birds seem very insignificant beside these exotic marvels, they have none the less the same significance for the participants. The White Wagtail circles round the female with legs bent, wings and tail spread horizontally and the feathers of the back bristling on end; the Blue-headed Wagtail stands erect to show off its yellow breast. The Red-backed Shrike, hanging on to a twig, sings whilst reaching backwards with the bill pointing towards the sky. The House-Sparrow hops up and down on one spot, wings hanging down, tail in the air, head sunk between the shoulders, and beak raised in order to expose the black throat. In the forest, the Black Woodpecker perched across a branch stretches its neck and swings it with a movement like a metronome; the Middle Spotted Woodpecker pursues his female with his red crest raised and forming a sort of cap.

Capercaillie uttering its 'song' (a clicking note) during courtship display.

Many species have nuptial flights which seem to play the same role as song, and are in some way intermediate between it and true displays, but which nevertheless often accompany them.

Three times in succession during a normal flight the Wood-Pigeon will rise rapidly, clap its wings, and then redescend in gliding flight; the Honey-Buzzard from time to time raises its wings vertically and shakes them; the European Sparrow-Hawk flies with slow and flexible wing-beats, spreading the lower tail-coverts which form white tufts at each side. It is during an ascending flight with vibrating wings, followed by a gliding descent, that the Curlew utters its most impressive song. The display flights

Emperor William's Bird of Paradise

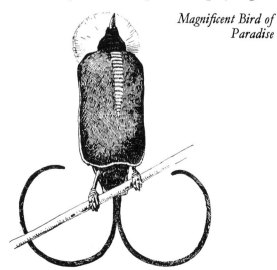

Magnificent Bird of Paradise

During the period of pairing and nest-building the Frigate Bird's throat is distended, forming an enormous sac which remains inflated even during flight and sleep. The throat does not revert to its normal state until the female has laid her eggs. In the foreground, a Red-footed Booby.

Courtship display of Ostriches. At the height of the display the male, crouching in front of the female, executes a rhythmical succession of movements with the wings and neck.

Left, display of Red-backed Shrike; right, courtship flight of Buzzard.

of the Serin and Greenfinch are well known and the Snow-Finch, which flutters in the same way while singing, interrupts its evolutions from time to time by a steep nose-dive towards the ground with a whistling of wings.

Where only the male displays he generally has a different plumage from the female, but when the two sexes are alike there are often displays in which the female takes an active part, sometimes equalling that of the male. Thus, as soon as winter is over, the Great Crested Grebes spend whole days in their rituals; facing each other, with necks stretched up, they remain motionless, only shaking their heads from side to side with jerky movements; at other times they run together on the water almost standing upright, sometimes holding each end of a stem. The same running on water occurs in the Divers [Loons] which also swim together on their backs, stomach in the air and head submerged.

The Wandering Albatrosses carry out a series of ceremonies, carrying material to the nest, clapping their beaks and calling;

at the finish of which they stand erect facing each other with their enormous wings outspread.

These mutual displays are also made during flight. They are common in birds of prey. Two Buzzards may describe large circles by flying one above the other when the upper one sud-

denly closes its wings and plunges towards the other which turns over to receive it; the wings open to brake the descent and the claws are hooked together for a moment before the two birds separate to start again. Ravens sometimes fly side by side almost touching as if yoked together,

Mutual display of the Great Crested Grebe. The two birds face each other with raised crests and shake their heads horizontally with jerky movements.

Display of Jackson's Whydah. With these East African birds each male makes a little circular arena by trampling down the grass around a central tuft. He dances by jumping round this tuft with his tail feathers spread in a very characteristic manner (top photograph). When a female arrives (centre photograph) he displays on the ground in front of her and the two birds remain one on each side of the tuft which they seem to be inspecting throughout the ceremony. In the bottom photograph the male, whose feathers have returned to their normal position, watches the departure of the female.

and do not alter this distance during lengthy evolutions.

Pursuit flights are quite common in many small birds—Passerines, Woodpeckers, etc. The male pursues the female, zigzagging or turning round the trees, and though this type of display does not seem very spectacular to us it nevertheless plays an important part in the life of the pair.

Various species of Penguins have rites, during the course of which they go through all sorts of motions interspersed with calls. Gulls also call and assume special attitudes, but, like Penguins and other species which nest in colonies, these displays, which are frequent between the two individuals of a pair, more or less occur in other circumstances and easily take on a character of social relationship. There is something similar in Oystercatchers when in various circumstances they gather together (from a pair

to ten individuals) and walk about with neck outstretched and beak pointed towards the ground uttering special calls.

The same applies to species which, without nesting in colonies in the proper sense of the word, remain more or less in parties (Avocets), but there is another type of collective demonstration which is found in far more solitary species which only gather together on such occasions. This is especially the case in a certain number of Grouse, in Europe the Black Grouse in particular. In places where they are numerous the males collect in spring before daylight on a common display ground, where each one has his own position, and engages in various gesticulations, wings hanging down, neck swollen, tail spread, appearing ready to attack its neighbour and to defend its position. There is sometimes a fight, but for the most part it seems to be nothing more than a sort of ritual, and serious combats are rare. When the females, attracted by the incessant cooing of the males, arrive on the ground, excitement increases, the males display by circling round them in a slightly different attitude, and copulation takes place. Almost identical behaviour is found in American species such as the Prairie Chicken and the Sage Grouse, in which gatherings of several hundred individuals have been observed. In other groups there are analogous assemblages but with a number of variations such as in Ruffs, certain Whydahs,

Birds of Paradise, Manakins, etc. Often, moreover, these gatherings continue when the females are incubating and no longer take part.

It is quite remarkable that a close relationship exists between the ornaments of the birds and the movements and attitudes of the displays. The ornaments and all the peculiarities of coloration and morphology are mostly used to make the general appearance of the bird as different as possible from the normal. Whether it be the simple black throat of the House-Sparrow, the long tapering plumes of the Common Heron, the extraordinary plumes of the Birds of Paradise, or the enormous wings of the Great Argus Pheasant, the position assumed by the birds is to show off these features to the best advantage. Even the Bluefooted Booby "goose-steps" to show off the colour of its feet, and the Fulmar gapes to show off the unexpected purple colour of the interior of the mouth.

The adaptation of movement to specialisations of plumage may be very highly developed. Thus many Birds of Paradise, which are closely allied and of the same general bearing, assume very different attitudes, each one displaying the ornamental plumes of the flanks according to their particular arrangement.

Quite often the bird basically does not seem to have any particular ornament to exploit. Thus displaying brings the gigantic wings of the Albatrosses and Condors into prominence, or the silvery breast of the Divers [Loons]. At other times flying prowess makes a contribution such as the acrobatic flights of the birds of prey.

It is in species where sexual dimorphism is most marked that the most extraordinary attitudes are found, bringing the special ornaments of the male into play. Further, in these birds the conjugal link is of very short duration, even if the union is not confined to copulation, as in the Grouse

Long-tailed Bird of Paradise; male at rest and displaying. The pectoral and flank plumes are raised and joined above the head forming a dark-brown, oval shield with a border of metallic violet. The tail is alternately spread and closed with rapid movements and from time to time the bird gapes, showing the yellow inside of its bill.

which display communally; it is here that natural hybridisation most often occurs (nevertheless always rare) in spite of the considerable external differences in appearance of allied species. In the promiscuity of meetings, the male may force copulation on a strange female, which does not occur in permanent pairs.

In any event, the attitudes in display are characteristic of the species; they make a sensitive chord vibrate, but this must be tuned in advance to be in resonance. A case in point is that of a male Black Stork and a female

The different species of Bower-Birds build varyingly shaped bowers. Some are quite simple like that of the Satin Bower-Bird of Australia (lower photograph), but the Crestless Gardener Bower-Bird of New Guinea (upper photograph) erects a veritable hut in front of which it places various objects, flowers, fruits, etc., of selected colours which it carefully keeps fresh.

White Stork which, under the artificial conditions of captivity, paired in a Zoological Garden. They were continually strange to each other because even after several years of communal life they did not understand the welcoming ceremonies at the nest which, though very simple, differ in each species, such as the clapping of the beak of the White Stork and the swinging neck of the Black Stork. The capacity for recognising specific motions is innate and cannot be acquired by training.

Display is, for the bird which carries it out, and much more for the one which witnesses it, a psychological stimulus which greatly influences physiological condition. It is not known exactly in which circumstances each sex needs the presence of the other in order to develop its reproductive cycle normally. It seems, from this point of view, that in the majority of cases the male is much more independent than the female, and that the psychological emotion produced in her by the presence of her companion is an important factor in her internal development.

The need of this visual stimulus and its effect have been evidenced by the female domestic Pigeon which does not lay when she is alone, but starts to lay if her cage is placed next to one in which a male is displaying. She may even lay if there is another female, or simply if she sees her own reflection in a mirror.

In many small birds with a

marked territorial behaviour, display attitudes are rarely specialised. The pair remains closely united; the constant presence of the male and his song, the offerings of food, and the carrying about of material constitute sufficient stimulus, so that the slightest abnormal manifestation of the male profoundly affects his companion. Hardly any characteristic displays are observed except during the formation of the pair and before copulation, and even these do not always regularly take place. They appear to be entirely lacking in some species, in the European Robin for example, where the only known attitude of display is that designed to intimidate a rival.

On the other hand there are groups where it seems that displays are necessary to establish and maintain synchronous conditions in the two mates, and which in some way also establish the permanent link of the group. This is particularly the case in the Great Crested Grebe, Herons, Penguins, and many birds nesting in colonies. In the latter, moreover, the presence of neighbouring pairs is a stimulus which may have considerable effect.

Displays attain their greatest development when the union of the two sexes is transitory. The males, which are usually very decorative, then dispense considerable energy, as the effect which they produce on the females, being of short duration, must be very intense in order to achieve its aim. This is the case in the Ruffs, certain Pheasants, Grouse, and Birds of Paradise, where many birds display together, and the males themselves appear to be stimulated by the displays of their neighbours. Other birds, like the Great Argus Pheasant, display alone, but their calls inform the neighbouring males, which reply; as, however, they remain at a distance there is no combat and the female may remain for several days in the company of the male.

It must be remembered that courtship displays are not confined to birds. Offering of food occurs in flies and spiders, and true displays are made by lizards, fish, certain insects, spiders, and even molluscs.

Barrow's Golden-eye. A male displaying, splashing up water behind it by thrashing out with its feet. Throwing up water with the bill or feet is quite a common feature in the display of several species of Ducks.

Reed-Warbler at nest.

Nest and eggs

Construction of the nest is a very specialised part of a bird's reproductive activities, but the ways in which it is done are very diverse, and practically all stages exist between the long and careful construction of very elaborate nests, and the establishment of simple improvisations hardly differing from other aspects of behaviour.

The female of the Red-throated Diver [Loon], who receives the male lying in a depression in the grass at the edge of the water, and remains there after his departure, then tears up moss which she throws behind her, without attempting to arrange it in any way, but at length this moss forms into a vague lining of the cup made by the bird's weight, and there the eggs are laid and incubated.

During the ceremonies of courtship display, the male of the Common Tern crouches before the female, then circles round her, and in order to remain facing him she also revolves, making a circular depression in the sand. At other times one of the two partners, bent forward, neck stretched, tail raised, throws the sand backwards with the feet. It thus digs a small cavity where the other partner at once goes, and

often repeats the same performance, after which stems of vegetation are brought ceremoniously. As the moment of laying approaches, these hollows become centres of attraction for the birds, and they progressively concentrate their whole attention on one of them, in which the eggs are deposited. During incubation the ceremony of nest-relief includes the bringing and arranging of materials. Finally a real nest may be constructed without any precise indication when the birds were engaged in a nuptial rite or the construction of a nest.

In the carrying about of material and scratching of ground with beak or feet, frequent during the

period of great sexual excitement, one is even able to see the origin of nest-construction. Actions which originally were no more than the expression of a momentary emotion, but resulting in conditions advantageous for the maintenance of the species (better protection for the brooding bird, eggs and young) are perfected by natural selection and result in the construction of a real nest.

Such a hypothesis is quite probable, the Common Tern being a good example among many others. Again it would be necessary to ascertain that the construction of a nest always followed the occurrence of gestures indicating sexual emotion, and that these

A pair of Pied Puffbirds near the arboreal termite nest where they have excavated their nest-hole. Brazil.

Male Penduline Tit building nest in a tamarisk. Camargue. The completed nest will be shaped like a purse with an opening at the side in the upper part just large enough for the birds to pass in and out.

are not "symbols" of building. There is no "fossil behaviour" which would permit the establishment of a chronology.

The impulse which leads a bird to build is primarily internal, and is manifested more or less clearly according to circumstances. One bird will carry material which it drops before actually building; another, in which the physiological condition is at the necessary pitch, will rapidly build a complicated nest. In particular, if a nest is destroyed, a new nest is always built very rapidly.

Though the construction of primitive nests may be merged with other activities and continue after the hatching of the eggs, that of the more complicated nests often begins under the influence of a sudden impulse; the nest is finished once and for all, and no further material is added.

In many birds which do not make nests, building activity is reduced to the choice of a site, and in certain sedentary species, where the conjugal link seems to be permanent, the same site may be used for several consecutive years, and at all times as a resting-place (Little Owl, etc.).

The actions accompanying the selection of the nest-site vary enormously according to the species and we have seen how, in the Terns, a depression in the sand becomes the final nest.

At the beginning of April, when

Sandwich Tern on nest. In this species moulting often begins very early, as may be seen from the first white feathers of the winter plumage on the head of this individual.

Bearded Vulture (Lammergeier) on its nest, typically located on a precipitous cliff with a steep drop below.

Nest of a Penduline Tit suspended from twigs of a tree.

Whereas many birds of prey ensure security for their nests by placing them in inaccessible craggy hollows, others build theirs at a great height in trees, like this Swallow-tailed Kite, a bird of the hot regions of America, whose nest is often over 100 ft. above the ground.

The ball-shaped nest of the Wren.

European Bee-eater perched in front of the slope in which the nest-holes of the colony are excavated.

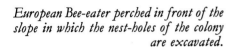

there are still few leaves on the trees, it is easy to watch a newly arrived pair of Wrynecks searching for the site of their future nest. Each hole in the trees is inspected, after which the two birds face each other at the edge of the hole, body erect, uttering their monotonous cry, and salute each other by swaying their necks. The choice always takes a long time, and they spend several days inspecting each section of their territory, ousting, if necessary, the Tree-Sparrows and Starlings already installed. It is often not until the end of the month, when the leaves hide them, that they finally select a hole for the nest. They both keep an eye on it during the day, then one of them spends the night there, and finally the eggs are laid shortly afterwards.

The choice may be made by one of the pair. Thus the male Pied Flycatcher, which returns first, establishes a territory in the forest and also inspects suitable holes.

The female starts to build immediately after her arrival, the male having indicated the chosen site by singing at the rim of the hole, quivering his wings, whilst his white chest makes a spot on the dark background.

In their neighbours the Stock-Doves, where the pair has already been formed for a long period, only the female chooses the hole in the tree during the course of long tours of inspection, followed by the male, who is content to display around her.

In many small Passerines, also,

Snow Petrel brooding on snow nest. Adélie Land, Antarctic.

the female makes the choice. From time to time she crouches in the fork of a branch or under a tuft of grass, and there, some time later, the nest is built. When the male is the first to return from migration, he may begin to build, even though the female does not always adopt what he has made, and may construct another nest elsewhere. Of course when the two sexes lead an independent existence, and do not meet except for nuptial rites (Ruff, Grouse, Humming Birds, etc.), the choice devolves on the hen alone.

The nest may be begun immediately the site is selected, or long afterwards—up to two months in certain sedentary birds which make the selection at the end of winter (Starlings, Tits). The role of the female in the construction is, as a general rule, the more important. Finding herself dependent on more distinct physiological conditions than the male, her activities are more clearly separated; the building of the nest, which seems more or less linked with ovulation, is for her

Two types of spherical nests:
Above, Fantail Warbler: Australia. Nest suspended in the grass. A few large leaves are tied on it by material worked through them like a button in a button-hole.
Below, Long-tailed Tit. As many as twelve youngsters can be reared in this nest which takes the parent birds several weeks to build.

a more imperious necessity than for her mate. He takes some part in the work, but very rarely builds entirely alone. Even in the Phalaropes and Dotterel, where the role of the sexes is partly reversed, the female takes part in the establishment of the nest, though a rudimentary one.

When the female builds alone, she is usually accompanied by the male, but he is content to remain near her. In certain Corvidae he also takes part in collecting material, and in some species is entirely responsible for providing it (Common Heron, Stork, Wood-Pigeon).

Usually, the nest is placed in sites which the bird habitually frequents, as a rule inside its territory. There are sometimes variations from one species to another; for instance the European Robin and Nightingale nest near the ground, but the Thrushes, which inhabit the same places and also find their food on the ground, nest in trees. There are other exceptions such as various Ducks (Carolina [Wood Duck], Mergansers, Golden-eye, etc.) which generally lay in holes in trees, often very high up; oceanic birds in the Arctic often nest several miles inland, sometimes at a considerable height.

The possibilities of movement also play a role; Divers [Loons], which can hardly move on dry ground, place their nests at the edge of water while that of the Grebes is floating. The Arctic Tern, on account of its particularly short legs, nests in much more exposed positions than the other Terns.

It is common for certain species to add material to the nest long after the period of incubation. Above, a female Montagu's Harrier taking a small branch; below, an Adélie Penguin bringing a pebble to its nest. The pebbles, which are sometimes very large, weighing up to about half a pound, may have been stolen from a neighbouring nest.

95

Common Heron bringing a twig to its nest.

The nest-site may vary according to local conditions; Cormorants, for instance, on the seashore nest on rocks, but when they inhabit lakes or rivers they build in trees.

As a general rule, security is the dominant factor in the choice of a nesting-site; for the nest must be completely protected from bad weather and predators. Many nests are concealed by the vegetation, and birds may nest later if the development of spring foliage is retarded. The nests of Reed and Sedge-Warblers, Little Bittern, Purple Heron, are above water, in the reeds. Others are placed in crevices in rocks, under stones, and in burrows. Some birds of prey and many sea-birds lay on the ledges of cliffs, the Magpie builds at the top of high trees. The Weavers and Caciques construct their pouch-like nests at the end of flexible branches, and the Palm Swifts attach theirs to the hanging leaves of palms. The protection given by prickly plants, acacias, cactus, yuccas, etc., chiefly in desert regions, has not been neglected. The Dipper sometimes makes its nest under a waterfall.

Protection may be strengthened by various associations. Though gregarious instinct is the chief

basis of nesting colonies, it is certain that security is increased by uniting numerous individuals banding together in common defence.

Small birds sometimes build within the actual structure of the nests of large birds of prey. In tropical countries, some take up their abodes in the neighbourhood of particularly aggressive birds, Drongos or Tyrants, who keep away predators; others build in the vicinity of dangerous insects, wasps, ants, or termites.

Man himself may be used, and in all countries his habitations are sought after by species which are hardly ever found in other places, such as Swallows, Martins, House-Sparrows. In tropical regions of the Old World certain Weavers live in the trees of villages, where they are less persecuted by raptors and snakes.

Protective associations form part of the normal behaviour of certain tropical species, but the chosen association may vary locally and even individually. Thus the Village Weaver, which in West Africa nests almost exclusively in the villages, has adopted the neighbourhood of

Left, nest of Sunbird in the web of a social spider. Ceylon. Association with creatures which are more or less dangerous is common among certain species of tropical birds. Right, nest of the Australian Rock-Warbler suspended by spiders' webs from the roof of a cave.

wasps' nests since its introduction into Haiti.

Associations of a somewhat different kind, but much more constant, exist between termites, or sometimes ants, and various

Female Capercaillie brooding.

Two types of rudimentary nests:
Above, Black-throated Diver [Black-throated Loon]. The legs are placed so far back that the birds can only drag themselves along the ground and therefore their nests are never more than a few yards from water.
Opposite, male Dotterel brooding; the female abandoned him immediately after laying the eggs and he will bring up the young alone.

birds, including Parrots, Trogons, Cotingas, Barbets, Kingfishers; for the nest is dug out of the interior of the colony of insects. The termites do not generally resist except a little during the excavation, and the bird, which does not feed on them, seems indifferent to their attacks. In the Trogons it has been observed that the hole was filled in by the insects after the birds had left. The Asiatic Rufous Woodpeckers which nest in the same way in arboreal ants' nests feed on their hosts, who despite this put up with them. It is difficult to understand how these associations, where all the advantages seem to be on one side, have come to be established, as the insect appears to be quite capable of evicting the bird.

Materials of animal, vegetable or mineral origin may be used for the construction of the nest, and the possibility of supply sometimes determines the habitat of a species.

Vegetable materials are the most general; small branches, twigs, and roots are often used in construction, twisted in each other by the movements of the bird's beak. Fresh or dried grass is also largely used, and some nests are entirely composed of it; dry grass may be moistened to soften it before being used. Sometimes whole tufts of short grass are torn up (Gulls). Leaves may be used as a support, as in the case of the famous nest of the Tailor Bird, which is placed inside a

Indian Paradise Flycatcher, male brooding. This type of nest, a small deep cup affixed to thin branches, is common among tropical Flycatchers.

House-Martin collecting mud for nest-building.

99

Female Red-breasted Merganser and nest on ground. The nests of Mergansers are also quite often placed in a hollow in a tree, even at a considerable height.

trumpet made of a large leaf rolled with the edges pierced by the bird which puts material inside, then pulls it through the holes and works it in such a way as to prevent the leaf from unrolling.

Vegetable down is used either for lining or for the construction of the nest itself. The felt of the Penduline Tit's nest is made in this way with nettle fibres, or wool, as a support. Some Humming Birds mix vegetable down with spiders' webs.

Dead leaves, moss, and lichens may constitute the fabric. Lichens added to the outside, and kept in position by spiders' webs, as in the Chaffinch, camouflage the nest so that it merges into the branch. In North America the Parula Warbler utilises the large hanging tufts of the usnea, or, in the south, those of the tillandsia, establishing a cavity in the interior, which it lines with bits of vegetation. Its distribution is correlated with that of these two plants. The Tree-creepers use the mycelium of fungi as an adhesive. Sea-birds use algae, which harden when dry, and weld the materials of the nest together.

Among animal matter, wool, down and hair serve as linings. Feathers are often taken from the places where birds of prey pluck their victims; Swallows and Swifts gather them in flight when they have been raised aloft by the draught caused by their wings. It must be specially mentioned that spiders' webs are used in very

Notornis or "Takahe" brooding. This large, flightless Rail was for a long time thought to be extinct. Recently some individuals have been rediscovered.

many nests, for their strength and adhesive qualities keep the other materials together.

Animal matter used in building may come from the bird itself, as for example in Swallows, Martins and Swifts, which have a particularly abundant secretion of sticky saliva at the time of building their nests. The nests of the Swiftlets —the "Swallows' nests" of the oriental gourmets — are almost entirely composed of this substance, at least those of some species; others also contain feathers and various vegetable matter. Other Swifts fasten together bits of vegetation and feathers with saliva to produce nests which are often simple but sometimes very elaborate like those of the *Panyptila* of tropical America. The minute nest of the Palm Swift is attached to leaves by the same method, and even the eggs are stuck to prevent them falling out. Some Humming Birds fasten their cup nest to its support in the same way, and the Golden Oriole with its saliva softens the vegetable fibres which fix the nest to the branches.

The down with which Ducks' nests are lined is taken by the female from her own breast, and the exploitation of Eiders' nests is well known.

Stones and bits of shell are often used to line the primitive nests of birds which build on the ground. But of all mineral matter earth is the most generally used. It is incorporated in some nests (Blackbirds, Thrushes, Magpies), it is used to build up the entrances of others, such as Nuthatches and Hornbills; it is either the sole constituent or is mixed with other materials in the nests of Swallows, Oven Birds, etc. Flamingos and some Albatrosses make a cup of dried mud.

Finally a most varied assortment of materials and objects seems to be used only for decoration; cast skins of snakes, pieces of paper, of fabric and so on.

The form of the nests is as varied as the materials. Only rarely is no foundation at all made; the Auks, however, lay their eggs on bare rock, and the Fairy Tern of the southern seas lays on a rock, the bole of a tree, or even in the fork of a branch.

A hollow in the ground, sometimes near a stone, or a tuft of grass, which gives some degree

of protection against the wind and sun, lined or not with various materials, may be considered as the rough outline of a nest. The next stage is a hole in the ground or in a tree.

Gulls, Gannets and Cormorants amass a fairly large pile of various materials formed into the shape of a cup. The birds of prey, when they build for themselves, do likewise; as they use the same nest several times, and continue to add branches, it may become of considerable size. For instance the nest of a Bald Eagle after twenty-five years of occupation reached a size of about twelve feet in depth and eight feet in diameter. In the course of time this mass of vegetable matter may ferment and produce humus, and it then forms a suspended soil colonised by insects and even earthworms.

Again, the nests of certain Passerines are constructed as simple cups — Corvidae, Nightingales, many Warblers—placed in vegetation or in holes, according to the species. The same type, but far more elaborate, is found in the nests of Finches and, in some (Chaffinch, Goldfinch, etc.), different materials are used for the main structure and for the internal

and external coverings. The cup itself is made by the bird, which revolves with the breast lowered, smoothing down the materials already put in position. Thrushes, which line the interior of their nests with mud, moisten their plumage before doing this. A further stage in elaboration is reached when the nest, unlike those already mentioned, is not placed between branches or stones, but suspended by its sides to the support. That of the Golden Oriole is supported on two sides, but the deep cup of the Reed-Warblers is attached to several vertical stems of reeds whose leaves prevent it from slipping. Other cup-nests are fixed to a bare branch — Humming Birds, various Flycatchers, etc. In the caves of South America, a near relative of the Nightjars, the Oil-Bird, places its mud cup-nest on a rock.

The mud nests of many Swallows and Martins and the cup-nests of the Swifts are often fixed on a vertical wall under a ledge of rock. That of the Red-rumped Swallow may be placed under the horizontal wall of an overhanging rock and the entry hole is preceded by a tube forming a corridor.

These cup-nests lead us to spherical nests with a lateral opening, such as those of the Long-tailed Tit, Wren and Dipper. That of the Rufous Oven Bird of South America is a great hollow ball of earth, fixed to a branch and weighing 7-9 pounds (the bird weighs less than 3 ounces). The nest of the Hammer-headed Stork, similar in shape, but made up of branches, is enormous in comparison with the size of the bird, and is the only example of this type of nest in the Ciconiiformes.

From the spherical nests which are placed on some form of support we pass on to the suspended pouches. The Penduline Tit makes its nest by first forming in the fork of a branch a sort of loop in the form of a hammock, which it enlarges before giving it definite shape.

The nests of the Sunbirds, and many other tropical birds, are loosely constructed pouches in which many spiders' webs are used; the long hanging nest of the Rock-Warbler is attached to the roof of the caves of Australia by spiders' webs.

The hanging nests of Weavers and Caciques are woven of grass and fibres, interlaced and knotted round the supports with very precise movements. Many Weavers first construct a spherical pouch, and the lateral entrance is then extended by means of a long passage which hangs downwards. The Caciques first construct the rim of the entrance, and then continue downwards in a long closed sack.

Numerous birds nest in burrows or holes in the ground. Many excavate these themselves: Puffins, Parrots, Kingfishers, and even Martins, which seem at first sight ill-adapted for such activities.

Holes in trees are more generally used than those in the ground. The bird may use the hole without any modification (Owls, Parrots, Rollers, Hoopoes, Trogons,

many as 2,000 feathers for the lining alone, and the construction of the whole nest takes them several weeks.

If the internal physiological condition of the hen plays a part in the start of building the nest, it seems that the sight of the finished work may influence the laying of eggs. In any event, this generally starts as soon as the nest is ready, and if this is destroyed before the clutch is complete, laying is suspended till a new nest is made—yet another example of the close relation between the bird's internal physiological condition and external factors.

In small Passerines one egg is laid each day, usually in the morning. In other groups the interval is variable, most often two or three days, but it may be as much as five or seven.

The number of eggs in a clutch is constant—within certain limits—in each species. Single eggs are fairly rare, but occur among the Auks, Procellariidae, the large Penguins, and a few other species. Many small Passerines have an average of from four to six, but the Tits may have as many as 15. Geese and Ducks often lay ten eggs at least; the gallinaceous birds also lay a large number (as

etc.), or enlarge it if the wood is soft (certain Tits, Barbets, etc.). Some birds excavate the holes entirely themselves. This is the case in Woodpeckers, which dig out of solid wood a hole, which at first is horizontal and then bends downwards. According to the species the bird may choose either healthy or partly decayed wood; in the American deserts the Flickers excavate holes in the giant cactus.

Some nests are simple and rapidly constructed, while others require a considerable amount of energy on the bird's part. A simple nest like that of the Redstart necessitates about 600 visits! The Long-tailed Tits collect as

Cup-shaped nest of Swallow made of dried mud reinforced with numerous bits of straw.

Hoopoe arriving at a hole in a tree in which the eggs are laid.

Stone Curlew about to settle on its eggs.

Clutch of Golden Plover eggs

Nest of Eider-Duck. The duck plucks the down from her own breast and, using her beak, lines the nest walls. Here one chick is already free of its shell, another is just hatching, while one egg seems to be still intact.

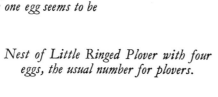

Nest of Little Ringed Plover with four eggs, the usual number for plovers.

many as 20 in the Common Partridge). There are, in addition, individual, and especially local, variations; the prevailing climatic conditions are also important, as well as the food supply.

If an egg is taken out of the nest before incubation has begun, the bird may lay an additional egg to compensate for the loss. If the removal of eggs is continued the laying may be considerably prolonged; for instance, in this way a Wryneck was induced to lay 62 eggs instead of the usual 8 or 10, and a Mallard is said to have laid a hundred or so. What then is the factor which causes the reabsorption of the numerous eggs still in formation in the oviduct when the normal number of the clutch is reached? Up to the present it has not been possible to find a definite answer to this question; it seems that the organism reacts to a visual perception—the relation between the size of the clutch and that of the nest rather than the number of eggs—or to the tactile perception of the eggs when the bird incubates. In any event this mechanism is only effective before incubation has commenced, for later on the bird either does not react, or abandons the nest if an egg is taken out. Not all birds, however, react in this way, for example, the Sandpipers and Gulls will not add to the clutch if an egg is removed.

When the whole clutch is destroyed another is laid in a new nest, sometimes very quickly; but the number of eggs in such replacements is generally reduced. The Procellariidae, the Albatrosses and some other species of fairly poor fecundity do not replace a lost clutch.

Many birds only lay one clutch a year, but certain small Passerines, especially in temperate regions, lay two or even three or four. The number varies in the same species according to local conditions; in high latitudes, with a very short period of good weather, only one clutch a year is possible for species which may lay several in other places.

The shape, texture and, above all, the markings of eggs vary. The average oval shape of the domestic hen's is the most general, but the eggs of Owls are almost spherical, those of the Nightjar elongated and equally rounded at both ends. The Guillemot's egg is distinctly conical, which enables it to revolve in a circle, and prevents it from rolling away if disturbed. Since the eggs are

Kiwi photographed in front of its egg which it has taken out of the burrow where it was laid.

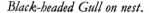

laid on bare rocks this characteristic considerably reduces possible loss by rolling over the edge.

The size of the egg obviously bears some relation to the size of the bird but there are considerable variations, and generally, in the same group the egg is proportionately larger in small species; for instance, 6 per cent of the total weight of the bird in the Albatrosses, 15 per cent in the Fulmar and 22 per cent in the Storm Petrels, all of which lay only one egg. The proportionately largest egg seems to be that of the Kiwi which is 25 per cent of the weight of the bird, and the smallest among living birds, that of the Ostrich (about 1·5 per cent), even though it is the largest in actual size (as much as three pounds or more). The smallest egg, that of a Humming Bird, weighs only half a gramme.

It is more interesting to compare the average weight of the clutch with that of the bird which lays it, for instance, the ratio varies from 3 per cent for the single egg of the Gannet to 120 per cent for the 11 eggs of the Goldcrest.

The bird may wait to complete the clutch before starting to incubate, and in such cases all the young hatch about the same

Eggs of Little Ringed Plover.

Nest and eggs of Reed-Bunting.

Nest and eggs of Eider-Duck with the down lining which is characteristic of all ducks' nests.

Eggs of Oystercatcher.

time; this is the general rule in the passerine and gallinaceous birds and the Anatidae.

In other birds, incubation begins during the laying of the clutch or even immediately after the first egg. As a result there is a difference in the time of hatching, and on account of their rapid growth there are considerable differences in size of the young birds, which may be fatal to those last hatched. This is frequently the case in Hawks and Owls.

The fact that a bird remains on the nest is not proof that incubation has begun; the feathers conserve the internal heat, so that an egg simply covered with them does not develop. Incubation is only properly effected by the "brooding spots" which the bird brings into contact with the eggs. These are areas varying in number—from one to three—where the down falls out, the skin becomes more delicate, the fat disappears, and a thick vascular layer ensures a high temperature. The temporary formation of these brooding spots is controlled by hormones. These spots are lacking in the Anatidae, Gannets and Cormorants. Penguins stand up when incubating, but a fold of skin of the ventral surface envelops the egg in a sort of pocket. Gannets cover the egg with their feet, the membrane of which is very vascularised.

Brooding spots only occur in individuals, whatever the sex, which actually incubate the eggs, for the task of incubation is divided differently according to the species. When both sexes take part in incubation. the male usually takes a smaller share than the female; in many gallinaceous birds, etc., only the female incubates. In the Button Quail, Phalaropes, Dotterel and some others, it is only the male.

When the bird comes to relieve its mate the change-over is frequently accompanied by ceremonies; the one which arrives often carries some small object, such as a twig or stone, and the one which is leaving throws behind it, over its shoulder, materials taken from the edge of the nest; in others there is bowing, movements of the wings, and various salutations. These ceremonies seem to be a ritualisation of gestures of appeasement, the brooding bird having a tendency to react aggressively on the arrival of another; in these ceremonies, also, as in the displays which precede nest-building there must be an expression of the link between the pair, an adjustment of their physical and psychological conditions.

In the small Passerines the incubating bird often leaves the nest for a few minutes in order to feed, but when only the female incubates she may be fed by the male. When both birds incubate, one may stay on the nest during the day, and the other during the night; in the Procellariiformes, which are eccentric in many ways, the relief takes place at intervals of several days, sometimes of several weeks, as in the Albatrosses. The bird which is not

Nest of Black Tern made of bits of dead reeds. ▶

sitting goes out to sea without any concern for its mate and traverses considerable distances; for instance, Manx Shearwaters found in the Bay of Biscay had a nest on the Welsh coast at the time they were captured. When only the female broods she in some instances hardly leaves the eggs during the entire period of incubation; the Eider-Duck may thus remain without food for twenty-eight days.

The first thing a bird does when it returns to the nest is to turn the eggs before settling down on them, and from time to time it raises itself to turn them again so that the distribution of heat is equalised. But, to judge from the behaviour of the Palm Swift, this turning is not always essential, for its eggs are glued to the nest.

The temperature of the egg during incubation seems to vary but little from one species to another and is on average 93° F. If incubation is temporarily abandoned, the cooling only affects the total length of incubation as the embryo can withstand relatively low temperatures (48° F to 52° F for a hen's egg). Though in temperate regions a rise in temperature has a bad effect on

Nesting mound of the Mallee Fowl in an arid eucalyptus forest in New South Wales (Australia). The female lays after the male has verified the temperature of the egg chamber where the eggs are laid with care, the point placed downwards.

Gull-billed Tern hatching. Camargue.

birds' eggs, in desert regions, on the contrary, they can withstand considerable rises; in some cases the adult birds even leave their eggs in the sun, more or less sunk in the sand.

The length of the incubation period does not depend on the state of development of the young bird on hatching, but more, though very approximately, on the size of the parent. It is generally about 14 days in the Passerines—with a minimum of 11—and it is hardly longer in the small gallinaceous birds. The Woodpeckers, whose development is very rapid, incubate only for a short time, also about two weeks—but Humming Birds, despite their tiny size, incubate for twenty-one days. The longest periods occur in the large birds; for instance it is nearly two months in the large Penguins and certain Vultures; whilst the Bearded Vulture (Lammergeier) and some Albatrosses take even longer. Cranes incubate for more than a month, and the Emu and Ostrich for a month and a half.

Up to now we have only taken into consideration the birds which incubate their eggs completely. Certain Ducks may abandon them during the last days, as the embryo begins to generate heat itself, but this is exceptional. On the other hand, in the forests of the Malay Peninsula, New Guinea and Australia, there is a small group of gallinaceous birds—the Megapodes—who do not incubate their eggs at all. Some species bury their eggs in the ground, sometimes in hot volcanic earth; others construct a pile of leaves and other vegetation mixed with sand, and the eggs are placed in a cavity excavated at the top of the heap and then covered with earth. These mounds attain a considerable size, for instance as much as 8 feet in height and 24 feet in diameter; the bird, which is hardly as large as a domestic fowl, may amass 5 tons of material which it scratches together from within a radius of several hundred yards.

The heat generated by the fermentation of the vegetation incubates the eggs without the aid of the parents in most cases. However, in the case of the Mallee Fowl of Australia, which has been closely studied, the male is busy with his artificial incubator for eleven months of the year. He prepares it four months in advance and does not allow the female to lay her eggs until the temperature inside the mound is just right. By a series of rather complicated processes, which vary according to local climatic conditions, he keeps the temperature of the eggs constant, the egg-laying being spread out over a period of several months.

The young birds reach the surface unaided and are independent immediately they hatch; they search for food on their own, are able to fly, and every evening—like many gallinaceous birds of the forests—perch on a branch for the night.

113

Egg and chick of Stone Curlew.

The young bird

If nothing occurs to disturb the long and inactive period of incubation, the eggs finally hatch and the life of the pair is suddenly changed.

The young bird emerges from the shell by breaking it from the inside, the tip of its beak being furnished with a temporary hard excrescence ("egg tooth") which it uses to pierce through the shell. The parents do not assist in this operation though Rails and Cranes, for instance, enlarge the hole already pierced by the chick.

At birth young birds can be divided into two categories—some are weak and blind, and remain in the nest till they are ready to fly—(nidicolous or altricial); others, on the contrary, are much more developed when they are born, are covered with down,

are fully able to see and hear, and can leave the nest almost at once (nidifugous or precocial). The extreme case is that of the Megapodes, which, from this point of view, have remained at the reptilian stage.

There are several intermediates between the two groups. Young Gulls for example, although they have the characteristics of nidifugous birds, are brought up in the nest; this avoids confusion among the chicks, as these birds often nest in very large colonies.

It is the appearance of the chicks which is responsible for the transition from the brooding to the feeding impulse in the parents. If the eggs do not hatch, the bird remains sitting much longer than the normal period. On the other hand, if the eggs are

replaced by young birds immediately after incubation has begun, they are accepted and fed at once.

Though the change is sudden, it is not always instantaneous and there are individual variations, the brooding bird going so far as to collect the scattered fragments of shell and sit on them again for some time. But this is rare, and, on the contrary, the parents often show signs of great emotion when the eggs hatch. Captive Sarus Cranes have been seen facing each other standing with their chick between them, gesticulating and making piercing cries as if to proclaim the news. When the female incubates alone, she may inform the male by special calls and flights, and he will at once care for the young. In other cases he must find them for himself, and although he may bring food

114

Lapwing chick.

The nests of Black-necked Grebe are generally in substantial colonies, often in association with colonies of Terns or Black-headed Gulls.

Curlew eggs hatching.

During the first two or three days of its existence the Flamingo chick, whose feet are swollen by a kind of oedema, stays at the nest before going to join the flock of other chicks which form a crèche looked after by all the adult birds.

Young Willow-Warblers begging for food.

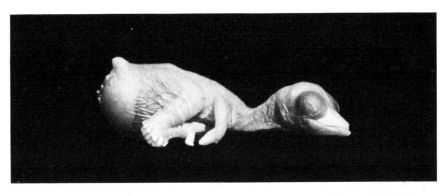

Development of a young Wryneck, a typical example of a nidicolous bird. At first the abdomen is distended and the limbs proportionately very small. On the heel joint are horny papillae which disappear as the toes grow. This characteristic is common in young birds which are reared in holes (Rollers, Woodpeckers, Toucans, etc.).

Just hatched (this photograph is enlarged twice as much as the others).

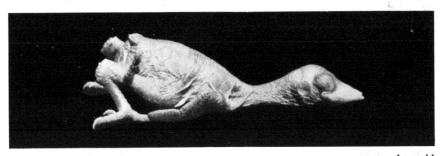

5 days old.

10 days old.

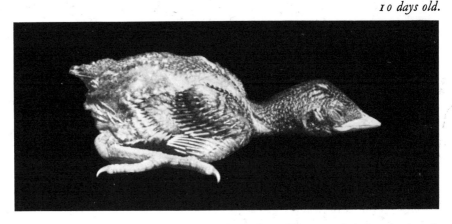

14 days old, one week before leaving the nest.

before the eggs are hatched, it may also be some time before he realises that the event has taken place.

When the brooding instinct is extinguished, the shells no longer have any significance for the parents, and are considered as rubbish to be got rid of. Many birds take them some distance away, others—Rook, Water-Rail, Barn Owl—smash them up or swallow them, or more rarely incorporate them in the lining of the nest; in the Flamingos the young bird itself swallows them.

It is curious that clear eggs, which are not hatched, sometimes remain, unless the movements of the young birds break them, and may be found intact after the youngsters have left the nest.

The famous case of the hen which was made to hatch out Ducks raises the question of the instinctive recognition of the young by the parents. The passerine birds will accept anything, including the parasitic Cuckoo, and do not seem to recognise their young individually until after they have left the nest.

The Herring Gull during the first four days accepts all the chicks of the same species and of the same age as its own, but after that

recognises them and kills any strangers that may be substituted. Later, when the chicks lose the nestling down and assume normal plumage, the parent no longer seems to recognise them, and they have to make special gestures of appeasement to be accepted. This gesture resembles that of the female at the time of the formation of the pair.

Chicks of domestic fowls have been reared, at least for a few days, by Owls or Buzzards, but in order to achieve this it was necessary for the birds to hatch them out themselves. Pheasants and Ducks, on the other hand, ignore or even kill young birds which differ too greatly from their own.

Immediately after they leave the nest, nidifugous birds follow the adult which guides them. In fact, experiments have proved that in some species they follow the first living being or even the first moving object that they see on hatching, for which they develop what may be termed a "fixation". In captivity this "fixation" may last for life and even sexual attraction may be focussed on the man, animal, or object

Chick of Purple Sandpiper. Lapland.

which the bird first saw. It is sometimes permanent, and the bird does not recognise the members of its own species, but frequently after a certain time these take on their normal significance. Analogous cases of "fixation" are found at other times in the life of a bird, and the different groups show this to a varying degree. Thus the young Fulmar immediately after hatching reacts aggressively to everything which appears suddenly near it; the parents have to arrive gently, chattering to calm it, and it is not till after three weeks that there is no more trouble, and in five weeks it at last recognises them.

Though the male sometimes plays only a small part during the period of incubation, he is more active in everything that concerns the care of the young and their feeding, and often plays as important a part as that of the female.

Exceptions are rare, and occur in species where the male maintains an individual territory more or less permanently, without taking any part in nest-building, such as species which are almost always polygamous — Grouse, Ruff, Lyre-Bird, etc.— as well as certain Ducks and many fruit-eating Passerines.

The female of the Red-breasted Snipe—the Robin Snipe or Dowitcher—which joins the male to incubate the eggs, leaves him alone after they have hatched, and goes off to form a flock with other females. The Phalarope, abandoned by his mate after she has laid the eggs, remains alone to bring up the young. The Rheas, which incubate the eggs of several females, and the Emus are in the same position.

In the Cranes each of the parents takes charge of a young bird. The Grebes share their duties in the same way, and it may

◀ *Nest of Dartford Warbler in gorse bush.*

happen, if hatching takes too long, that one of the pair goes off with the first chick, and the other with the second, without waiting for the birth of the rest.

The males of certain birds of prey hunt and bring back their prey to the nest, but the female alone dismembers it and distributes the pieces. If the female dies at the beginning of the rearing of the young, they will perish beside a supply of food which their father is incapable of preparing for them. If they are older, however, they will tear off bits for themselves; this stimulates the male, who then sets about distributing some morsels and the brood may be saved.

The Hornbills, which have such strange adornments on the beak, have very peculiar habits. They nest in holes in trees and close up the entrance with mud mixed with pieces of vegetation or their own regurgitated pellets. When the opening is only just large enough for the female to enter, she installs herself in the hole and continues to reduce the aperture until there is only a chink sufficient for the point of her beak to emerge. During the whole period of incubation she is fed by the male, who, after the eggs have hatched, continues to supply her with food which she gives to the young. In the large species, when the young are capable of flying the wall is broken down from the inside by the female, who, incidentally, has moulted during her incarceration. In the smaller species with more numerous offspring, she comes out sooner, and takes part in feeding them; in this event the wall is often restored by the eldest of the young birds and is finally demolished when they leave fifteen days later. During the time the birds are in the nest it is kept scrupulously clean, the excrement being thrown out.

In the Passerines, feeding is usually shared equally by both parents, but in spite of this they have to expend considerable energy. For example, Tits have been known to make nearly 400 visits to the nest in a single day, the frequency reaching 72 trips in an hour. It is the opposite in the Albatrosses and Tropic Birds which only feed their young once a day.

When the adult arrives at the nest, the young stretch their necks, swing their heads, and open their beaks wide. At first, when they are still blind, this instinctive movement is released

The eyes of these young Ring-Ouzels are not yet fully opened. Their necks are stretched vertically but soon will be turning in the direction of the parent's bill.

by the noise, or movement of the nest, produced by the arrival of the parent. Later, it is the sight of the food provider which causes the begging gesture, and the neck is no longer stretched up vertically but towards the arriving bird.

The beak of the young bird has a light-coloured border forming a thick rim, which when opened is diamond-shaped, and as the interior is often decorated with coloured papillae the whole effect is very striking, and acts as a

Female Bearded Tit at nest. In this species the coloured papillae in the young bird's throat are very conspicuous.

Little Bittern. The female is disgorging a small fish into the chick's throat. Little Bitterns are very small herons, and some of the exotic species are scarcely larger than a Blackbird.

powerful stimulus on the parents to provide food. This instinctive gesture is released in such an automatic manner that sometimes a bird passing near the nest of a stranger, and seeing the young open their beaks, stops and gives them the beakful of food it was taking to its own nestlings. In the same way it has been possible to make birds "feed" artificial beaks in order to study the composition of the provender distributed.

It might seem that this mech-anical distribution favours the bird which is best placed, to the detriment of its brethren. Actually the disposition is perfectly adapted to an equal distribution because, if for some time one of the nestlings receives more than the others, it is quickly gorged and falls asleep at the bottom of the nest to digest its food; another then takes its place, later to fall asleep in its turn. It is only in certain birds of prey, where hatching is spaced out over a long time, that the last to be born may be at a disadvantage, kept in the background by the more active older birds, and it may even perish. The young of the European Kingfisher exhibit a quite exceptional and peculiar instinct. At the beginning, when they are still weak, they open their beaks automatically when the adult arrives. This reflex is released, as in young Woodpeckers, by the obscuring of the hole at the entrance to the nest. But, when they are able to move about, they range themselves in a circle one behind the other, and when the

House-Martin. Here a young bird sufficiently developed to be ready to leave the nest comes to the entrance to receive food from the parent bird.

122

one which is in front of the entrance has received its share, the whole family turns in such a way that the next one in its turn moves into position at the place of distribution.

The Passerines put the food direct into the youngster's throat. When the Great Tit has captured a large caterpillar or big spider it squeezes it to extract the liquid, which it distributes to several young, and then swallows the rest. The Cotingas behave in the same way with fruit.

Storks, Herons and Gulls place the food they bring in front of the chick. Albatrosses, Petrels and Shearwaters regurgitate food straight into the young bird's mouth and Humming Birds do likewise, plunging their beaks as far down as the oesophagus. It is the opposite in Pelicans, Cormorants, Gannets and Penguins, and the young bird plunges its head into the mouth of the adult to procure its food from the throat.

In certain Pigeons, as for instance in Wood-Pigeons, domestic Pigeons, and closely allied species, there is a very specialised peculiarity in both sexes, the inner side of the crop thickening and secreting a liquid which the young bird obtains from the parent's throat. At first this "milk" constitutes the sole nourishment but later it is mixed with regurgitated food; its formation is controlled by prolactin, the same hormone of the hypophysis which excites the secretion of milk in mammals. The crop begins to produce this milk shortly before the eggs are hatched, which explains why Pigeons differ from other birds, and abandon the clutch if the eggs do not hatch at the normal time.

The food of the young is usually about the same as that of the adults, but often food is given after having been some time in the parent's crop or stomach where it is saturated with digestive juices. The seed-eating Passerines also give their young a large number of insects.

Though feeding forms the largest part of the parents' activity during the rearing of the young, their duties do not end there, for the chicks need further care in order to survive. The internal temperature of the weak and naked nidicolous birds on hatching is hardly above that of the surrounding medium, and at this stage they behave like cold-blooded animals. The thermoregulatory mechanisms do not begin to function for several days and in the Passerines it is only towards the ninth day that they are fully developed. One of the adults, therefore, has to brood the young during this period, otherwise they would perish, and even later they have to be protected from undue cold or rain, the more so if the nest is unsheltered.

Young Woodpeckers squatting at the bottom of their deep nest seem to be left to themselves without any ill effects more often than other birds.

During bad weather young Swifts which their parents are no longer able to feed fall into a state of lethargy, during which their temperature may fall at night as low as 70° F, though it reverts to normal during daylight hours. With the cessation of fasting, which they can endure for ten days, they rapidly return to their normal condition.

In the Antarctic the Emperor Penguin nests in the depth of winter; the young are kept between the adults which form a compact mass round them during blizzards, but despite this, losses are very severe.

If cold is fatal to young birds, an excess of heat is no less so. A scantily covered Passerine soon dies in full sunshine if one of the parents does not shelter it. This phenomenon has been observed mainly in birds which have exposed nests; Herons have even been seen cooling their young by fanning them with their wings. In birds which nest on the ground in regions of intense heat, certain Saharan species among others, it is difficult to understand how the young birds, even if sheltered from the direct rays of the sun, can endure the temperature of the ground, which at certain times exceeds the limit fatal to birds.

In nidifugous species the body temperature of the young is established at birth and they do not

Red-throated Diver with two chicks, the usual number for Divers.

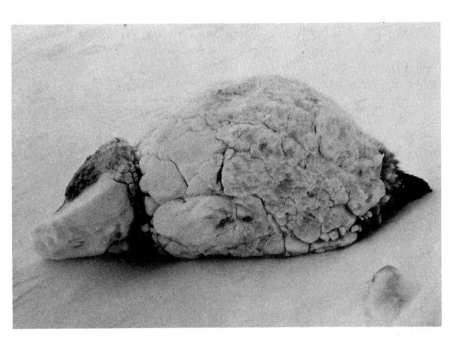

Young Adélie Penguin encrusted with a coating of frozen snow after a blizzard.

need to be kept warm except for a short time before leaving the nest. Nevertheless they take refuge under the wings of the adults in bad weather or for the night. Their energy varies according to the species. The Grebes hardly swim at all during the first few days, but are carried on the backs of the parents, nicely warmed among the feathers, and are also fed there. Ducks, which are more active, swim after their mother immediately they are led to the water, and in some cases, after having jumped out of a nest situated several yards above the ground. Two days after hatching, a young Curlew was found two miles from the nest, and the day after birth Greenshanks are conducted to the feeding grounds, sometimes more than a mile from the place where they are born.

In a nest where there are a number of birds crowded together, there must be strict sanitation and the excreta removed if

Oystercatcher removing eggshells from the nest.

Whitethroat removing parasites (?) from the nest.

developed it ejects its excrement on the edge of the nest, and the adult takes it away; the consistency is such that it leaves no trace; in the Lyre-Bird the faecal sac is projected into the air and seized in flight, being subsequently disposed of in water or buried in the ground.

The parental instinct may lessen or disappear during the last days the nestlings remain in the nest. Thus, when young Goldfinches leave the nest, its edge is coated with a white crust. Young Swallows drop their excrement outside, and the pile which accumulates below has no ill effect on the nest, which is always situated far above.

In certain Parrots which nest in holes, the faeces may either be sufficiently dry to cause no trouble, or be destroyed by a special fly and its larvae; this latter method is found in other species, especially in the Trogons. The young Nightjar, which hatches from an egg incubated

the occupants are to survive. This is achieved in the Passerines by the secretion in the cloaca of the young bird of a gelatinous envelope which covers the excrement. When the chick has been fed, it turns round and the adult seizes the faeces which are then passed; if the young bird does not void spontaneously, the parent incites delivery by tickling the region of the anus or tugging the down. At first the faeces are swallowed by the parent; later they are taken out and dropped at some distance. When the young bird is further

'Frozen' position of a Little Bittern on its nest. The attitude is instinctively adopted, even if, as here, the camouflage is not effective. The very mobile eyes continue to look forward. ▶

Young Great Crested Grebe sheltering on the parent bird's back.

Bullfinch distributing food to its young

Squacco Heron regurgitating food. The nestling seizes the beak of the parent bird, which inclines its head sideways so that the food can drop into the chick's throat.

Female Hen Harrier feeding her young.

An Imperial Eagle of the Spanish sub-species. The female is offering food to a nestling which, judging by its distended crop, appears to be replete.

Barn Owl nesting in a hay-loft.

Little Ringed Plover chick among pebbles on a river-bank and Golden Plover chick on lichen-covered ground in Iceland (above); the coloration of the down makes them both very difficult to see when motionless.

Water-Rail removing unhatched egg from nest.

directly on the ground, is sufficiently active to move about, but instinctively remains tied to the exact spot where it is born. It moves a short distance away to excrete, making a white circle in the middle of which it is fed.

Though in the Passerines the neighbourhood of the nest remains undisturbed and does not give away its position, a heronry is seen from afar, as all the surroundings are whitened by the spurts of liquid projected outside the nests. It is often the same with the Raptores; in the vicinity of a nest of the Goshawk or European Sparrow-Hawk, branches fouled by the young or adorned with the moulted feathers of the female may attract attention from a distance. It is well known how, on the Peruvian coasts, the celebrated deposits of guano are formed by immense colonies of sea-birds, especially Cormorants. Conditions which would soon lead to the death of small species with deep thick nests are of no

Linnet removing droppings from nest.

Behaviour of Avocet whose nest is threatened. Opposite: Feigning injury. It leaves the nest limping with one wing outstretched. Below: Intimidation display.

importance when the birds are reared in more open nests, and have hardly any fear of predators.

The whole time that the young are dependent on their parents, their own defence against danger is chiefly passive. During the first few days it does not exist at all, and any disturbance that they are capable of perceiving only produces in them the reflex of demanding food. But a time arrives, and the transition is usually sudden, when they distinguish the arrival of anything different from the parents, and react by flatten-ing themselves motionless at the bottom of the nest. Later they may even leave the nest and hide in the nearby vegetation.

The nidifugous chicks, able to see and hear on hatching, have the innate faculty of perceiving even distant danger, as, for example, a bird of prey in flight; they also respond instinctively to the alarm calls of their parents, remaining motionless where they are with their eyes closed, and the colours of their downy plumage generally merge so well into the surroundings that they become practically invisible.

Cryptic colorations also occur, though in general to a much lesser degree, in the first plumage of nidicolous birds. When the adult male is brightly coloured the young bird is drab, and more or less similar to the female. It is only in the birds that nest in holes, where the young remain invisible till they leave, that the juvenile plumage may be similar to that of the adult (Woodpeckers, Kingfishers, Parrots, etc.).

Active reactions are quite rare in young birds; young Hawks and Owls may lie on their backs and threaten with claws and beak; the young Fulmar and all other Procellariiformes eject, as soon as they are born, a bad smelling oil which is characteristic of the group. It is curious that this reaction occurs in some young Albatrosses, though it is unknown in the adult.

A bird which is brooding or bringing up its young has quite different reactions to danger from when it is alone. The specific and individual differences, and the variation in relation to the stage in the reproductive cycle, are considerable. Some only utter a cry of alarm, others attack the intruder, and in this case it is not

Reed-Bunting. Threat display and attack by female on returning to nest and finding brown rat after her eggs.

always the most powerful birds which show the greatest boldness. But the most interesting of all these reactions is that which can be called, though not always very appropriately, injury feigning. This fact has been noted since ancient times—Aristotle mentioned it—and Buffon describes the behaviour of a Partridge in front of a dog as follows: "The male was seen to take flight, but clumsily and dragging a wing in order to attract the enemy with the hope of an easy prey, always going fast enough not to be caught, but not so fast as to discourage the pursuer, drawing it further and further away from the brood." Whether the injury is well imitated or not, it is certain that the procedure is effective and numbers of predators are drawn away from the young in this manner.

It is evidently not conscious strategy on the bird's part. Specialists in animal psychology have especially studied the problem and it seems that characteristic reactions emanate from two opposing tendencies: flight in order to ensure personal security, aggressiveness to ensure security of the young or nest. As in many

similar cases, it is not a compromise between the two tendencies which results, but the appearance of a different reaction. A number of facts supports this interpretation. Thus injury feigning only occurs when the young are threatened; a bird which is at a distance from the nest and only fears for itself reacts in the normal way. Likewise if the danger only affects the brood—attack by a rodent, Magpie or Jay which are not the normal enemies of the adult—the parents react by attacking the predator. The more sudden the danger the more

intense is the reaction; if the bird is aware beforehand of the arrival of an assumed enemy, it will even hide after having warned the young by alarm notes.

It seems that in certain birds the reactions are to some extent ritualised: they are manifested regularly, their frequence varies in accordance with the reproductive cycle, and they become true distraction displays; it is in these cases that the most successful imitations are observed. But they may take other forms, also advantageous for the preservation of the species. Some birds

Sandwich Tern protecting its young.

(Oystercatcher, etc.) unobtrusively slip off the nest and go away to "brood" ostentatiously somewhere else, or "sleep" with the head under the wing, or begin to preen.

The rapidity with which the young grow is unique among the vertebrates and reaches its maximum intensity in the nidicolous birds. A young Cuckoo which weighs $\frac{1}{14}$ of an ounce at birth weighs fifty times as much three weeks later. A Common Heron, weighing $1\frac{1}{2}$ ounces on hatching, weighs three and a half pounds, about thirty-eight times its original weight, at the end of forty days. During the same time a rabbit of equal weight at birth only reaches a weight of just over a pound. In nidicolous birds there is a lack of co-ordination, the digestive organs—especially the liver and intestine—being very advanced compared with the limbs and sense organs. Metabolism is so intense that there is a rapid accumulation of reserves, which subsequently serve to complete development. The young bird at some stage may even weigh more than its final weight; the chick is heavier than the adult. Thus a Pelican which weighs about thirty-one pounds when 63 days old weighs about nine pounds less 40 days later; a Swallow which weighs $\frac{13}{16}$ of an ounce when 15 days old does not weigh more than $\frac{5}{8}$ of an ounce at three weeks. The phenomenon is very marked in the Procellariiformes—Albatrosses, Petrels, etc.—in which the young bird, abandoned without food when reared, completes its growth by using up its reserves of fat. The Manx Shearwater remains like this for ten days before flying, and the Wandering Albatross up to three months.

Growth is also rapid in nidifugous birds but without any marked lack of co-ordination, which is probably the result of their regular muscular activity.

This high rate of growth necessitates the provision of a considerable amount of food. Young Starlings and Crows after hatching consume the equivalent of half, and, after a few days, almost the whole, of their own weight in food.

The psychic faculties and various instinctive actions gradually appear during the growth of a nidicolous bird. As has already been stated, certain behaviour elements, such as the fear reflex, may appear suddenly, and then mature during the course of growth.

Young Owls of the same brood hatched on different dates show distinct differences in size; in the larger of these two Eagle-Owls the flight feathers have already appeared.

It might appear that when the feathers of the wings of the young are fairly well developed they "learn" to fly by exercising their wings on the edge of the nest. Actually the movements of flight are innate and do not have to be learnt, but this instinct appears only gradually, and, to start with, the movements are badly co-ordinated and would not achieve successful flight. Pigeons which were prevented from using their wings until others of the same age were able to fly normally also flew equally well when liberated. Only the precision of flight, chiefly alighting, seems to need some practice.

The time of leaving the nest varies in different groups, but is fairly constant in any given species, if nothing abnormal has occurred during the rearing of the young. Small Passerines remain in the nest for about two weeks, the Raven for five or six. Certain groups are very precocious; the Woodpeckers, for example, may leave the nest at three weeks of even less (Green Woodpecker) and the largest (Black Woodpecker) at four weeks. The Swifts, on the other hand, in spite of their quite small size, remain in the nest for six weeks, which is connected with the exceptional development of their faculties. It seems that the young bird, which launches itself into space on its first appearance, immediately leaves on migration. The Procellariiformes, which are in somewhat the same position, also remain in the nest for a long time—60 days in the Storm Petrels in spite of their small size, and nearly six months in the large Albatrosses.

Birds of prey leave the nest very late. For example, small Falcons leave at the end of a month, the Golden Eagle after two months, the large Vultures three months, and the rare Californian Condor not for six months or more.

The impulse which makes the young birds leave the nest may appear very early, well before they are able to fly, especially in species whose nests are situated near the ground. As their feet are better developed than their wings, they can move about and scatter, thus diminishing the risk of the destruction of the whole brood by predators. The parents are guided to feed them by their calls, and gather them together if necessary in cold weather to warm them. This behaviour occurs as much in the Passerines as in groups like the Herons, where young Bitterns, whose feet enable them to walk about among the reeds, make excursions round about the nest after one or two weeks, and finally leave it well before they are able to fly.

When the nest is situated very high up, or is very deep, the young birds do not leave till they are completely developed. Some leave of their own volition, others have to be encouraged by their parents, who may stop feeding them, or on the other hand, bring food and offer it to them without letting them take it.

The Guillemots and Razorbills are an exception to this rule. Reared for two weeks on the rocky cliffs of the Atlantic, the chicks, still covered in down and with hardly any feathers in their wings, one evening throw themselves into the water from very great heights. Drawn by the ritual displays of their parents, they precipitate themselves over the edge of the rock on their own, their little vibrating wings slowing down the fall. If they fall straight into the water this movement does not stop, and they dive and come up again out of the surf. If they fall on to a rock they are usually unharmed, as the

Adélie Penguin with chick.

Almost from birth Bitterns, when alarmed, camouflage themselves by pointing their beaks vertically, parallel to the reeds.

Griffon Vulture and young at nest.

The Tawny Owl nearly always nests in a hole in a tree but, exceptionally, as here, uses a nest previously belonging to another bird.

◄ Little Egret with young ready to leave the nest.

Young Great Crested Grebe already full grown but still partly retaining the characteristic striped plumage of the chick.

down and a thick layer of fat break the fall. They drink a lot at first. The rocks, which are teeming with life one evening, are deserted the next day, as all the birds leave at the same time, and it may be that emulation plays a part in this drastic exodus.

After they have left the nest, the young birds are still fed and protected for some time. Families may remain united and leave together on the autumn migration or, on the other hand, mix up with other birds, and later form into large winter flocks.

Others disperse, and the young birds establish themselves far from the parental territory. Some-

times they form independent parties; some Bustards form into flocks of males or females which live separately.

Sometimes young birds show signs of reproductive behaviour. Some Weavers build nests; young Coots, Moorhens [Gallinules], Swallows and Martins sometimes help their parents in feeding a second brood; and the two latter species have even been known to sit on the eggs or warm the newly born nestlings. However, in this case, it may perhaps be more a desire to shelter in the nest where they were reared rather than premature appearance of a phase of reproductive behaviour.

Yonng Cuckoo still not able to fly, but already too big for the Reed-Warbler's nest in which it was reared.

Cuckoos and other parasites

Under the term parasitism it has become the practice in the animal kingdom to include somewhat diverse habits ranging from simple commensalism to symbiosis. Birds, alone among the higher vertebrates, exhibit a behaviour which may be designated by this term, and this only comprises parasitism during reproduction, one species devolving upon another more or less completely, the duty of rearing its young. The Cuckoo is one of the most perfect examples.

In spite of numerous studies, there is still no general agreement on all the phases of its behaviour, which seem to show not only variations, but an almost disconcerting lack of precision.

On their arrival in spring, males and females establish separate territories, which are not always very well defended, and that of the male may overlap those of several females. There would seem to be no established pair, but, on the contrary, a certain promiscuity, comprising either polygamy or polyandry.

Ovulation seems to be stimulated in the female by the sight of the nest in which she will deposit her eggs, and her great occupation is searching for these nests. She watches the building of them, and if she finds a nest where the clutch is complete before she herself is ready to lay, she may take out the eggs so that the owner will continue to lay and not start incubating too soon. Even the entire clutch may be destroyed, resulting in the construction of a new nest. Thus the Cuckoo, once she is "ready" to lay, almost always has at her disposition a nest which is "just right".

The eggs are laid at intervals of two days, usually in the afternoon. The manner in which they are placed in the nest varies according to circumstances. In an open cup-nest the bird lays directly into the nest; if there is a lateral opening, she finds the means of ejecting the egg through it. The possibility of the egg being laid on the ground and then transported and deposited in the nest has been disputed, but some observations seem sufficiently conclusive; in any case it is difficult to understand how eggs could be laid in the nest of

Cuckoo's egg in the nest of a Marsh-Warbler.

the Fantail Warbler, which is so lightly constructed, and only supported by vegetation which would not bear the weight of the Cuckoo. Often, either at the actual time of laying, or soon afterwards, an egg of the fosterer is taken away.

Although small birds treat the Cuckoo more or less as an enemy, mobbing and chasing it on every possible occasion, many do not take any notice of the strange egg in their nest, but reactions vary according to species and individuals, and the Cuckoo's egg may be thrown out, or the nest abandoned or even destroyed.

In the Wood-Warbler an average of 67% abandoned nests has been recorded, but only 12 to 14 % in the Fantail Warbler.

If the egg is adopted it usually hatches before the young of the fosterer, as the incubation period is a day or two shorter.

During the first four days of its existence the young Cuckoo has a cavity in its back where the skin is particularly sensitive. As a result it instinctively throws out of the nest everything which comes into contact with this sensitive area. The eggs of the fosterer, or the young if they are hatched, are thus thrown out one

by one, and the Cuckoo remains in sole possession.

It stays in the nest for about three weeks and continues to be fed quite a long time after leaving it.

The behaviour of the Cuckoo is therefore adapted to that of its fosterers and takes full advantage of the weak points in their reproductive instincts, which in ordinary circumstances would have no ill effects. These weak points comprise:

—continuing to lay when an egg is taken away;

—laying in the morning and leaving the nest unprotected

The young Cuckoo, hatched before the young of its foster-parents, ejects the eggs from the nest.

Two African Cuckoos:
a) *Klaas's Cuckoo* (Chrysococcyx klaasi);
b) *Emerald Cuckoo* (Chrysococcyx cupreus)
and a few of their hosts:
c) *Scarlet-chested Sunbird* (Cinnyris senegalensis);
d) *Paradise Flycatcher* (Terpsiphone viridis);
e), f) *Male and female Village Weaver* (Ploceus cucullatus). ▶

during the afternoon, thus enabling the Cuckoo to lay without being disturbed;

—acceptance of a strange egg which is often not distinguished from the others;

—not recognising the young of another species;

—indifference during the feeding period to anything that is not inside the nest, which makes them oblivious of the young ones thrown outside;

—automatic feeding of an open beak; that of the Cuckoo, which is orange bordered with yellow, seems to be especially stimulating in this respect.

Further the Cuckoo, which is insectivorous—it eats many hairy caterpillars which other birds will not touch—is parasitic on species which give their young appropriate food. If an egg is laid in the nest of a seed-eater the young bird is thin, as it does not get sufficient animal food.

The species on which the Cuckoo is parasitic are very numerous, but many are only used adventitiously. In Europe the most usual are Pipits and Wagtails, some Warblers—chiefly the Reed-Warblers — Robin, Wren, etc.

Robin feeding a young Cuckoo.

Theoretically, each female is only parasitic on the species by which she has been reared and on which she has formed a "fixation" during her youth. Specialised strains of Cuckoos would therefore be established which would adapt their eggs to the colour of those of their fosterer. This fact would be easy to explain by the action of automatic selection, since the more the egg resembles that of the fosterer the better the chance of it being adopted, and therefore of the survival of the race. It is evident that, on the whole, the colour of Cuckoos' eggs varies a great deal, but each female—this is not restricted to parasites—lays eggs of the same type. Though this adaptation, which may even apply to the size, seems to be realised in certain regions and in certain birds, it cannot be laid down as an absolute rule.

It would take too long to enter into the details of the discussions which the problem has aroused, and a few examples will show the difficulties which it presents. In Finland there is a predominance of Cuckoos with blue eggs which are parasitic on the Redstart, which also lays blue eggs; in Japan the eggs have the same vermiculations as those of the Buntings on which the Cuckoo is parasitic; in Hungary there is a marked adaptation to the Great Reed-Warbler which is practically the only fosterer. On the other hand, in Algeria the Cuckoos, which always lay blue eggs, are often parasitic on Moussier's Red-

start which sometimes lays blue, and sometimes white eggs. In France the Wren is the most usual fosterer, and no adaptation has been established, the eggs—larger than those of the fosterer—being variable in colour.

The problem is far from being solved, in spite of the attention paid to it by specialists—one of whom collected nearly 4,000 clutches containing Cuckoos' eggs—and the irregularities of other phases of behaviour, as well as difficulties of observation, increase its complexity.

The imperfections of an adaptation, remarkable as it is, result in a very high percentage of losses, 30 to 40 % before leaving the nest. In addition, the young bird, which for a long time remains dependent on its foster-parents for food, is very vulnerable. It is therefore necessary for the species to lay a fairly large number of eggs, and the female lays at least a dozen (as many as 26 in one case). This number is correlated with the fact that in parasitic birds there is no incubation to limit the clutch. However, the figures recorded have been made by observers who collected entire clutches. Further, it is not certain that the female does not watch the rearing of her young (though taking no part in this), and therefore may be influenced by the new nests made by her victims in order to replace the lost clutches. In consequence the figures obtained cannot be accepted as typical.

Many Cuckoos have a normal

reproduction, but parasites are numerous, especially in the Old World. First there are the close relatives of the European Cuckoo (genus *Cuculus*) which all have very similar habits. The small metallic Cuckoos of the Indo-Australian region and Africa have very diverse fosterers, and it seems that the males sometimes feed the young after they have left the nest. The Great Spotted Cuckoo, a species which occurs in the south of Europe, lays its eggs mainly in the nests of the Corvidae, such as the Magpie in France, the Spanish Blue Magpie in Spain, Crows, etc. The young do not possess the dorsal cavity and are brought up together with the legitimate brood. There are also other genera with parasitic habits, but details are lacking for many tropical forms. In America the only parasite among the Cuculidae seems to be the Striped Cuckoo, but the family Icteridae contains a large number of different examples. Thus the Bay-winged Cowbird, which frequently takes possession of the nests of other birds in which to bring up its young, is largely victimised by the Screaming Cowbird. Another species of the same genus, the North American Cowbird, is the best known parasite in that continent. It lays eggs in the nest of many other Passerines.

In the family Ploceidae, the Whydahs, which are polygamous, are parasitic. Their fosterers are almost always Waxbills, whose eggs are also white, and the young are brought up together. There are certain striking resemblances between the juvenile plumage and the interior of the beak of the parasitic bird and its usual fosterer, though the adults differ in appearance. Moreover, the male Whydah's song is made up of motifs peculiar to itself combined in variable proportions, according to circumstances, with those of the species on which it is parasitic.

In Africa the Honeyguides are especially parasitic on Woodpeckers and Barbets.

Whilst more or less well devel-

Parasite Whydah and Waxbill; left to right: Whydah adult male, young; Waxbill young, adult male.

oped parasitic tendencies exist in very different groups, these are usually restricted to taking possession of a nest. We will only mention the Black-headed Duck of South America which lays in the nests of other Ducks, or sometimes in those of Coots, Gulls, etc. The chicks for a day or two receive care and attention from their fosterers, but thereafter lead an independent existence. This is the only case known of well-marked parasitism in birds with nidifugous young.

Reed-Warbler sheltering a naked young Cuckoo (which is not visible) from the sun.

147

Chapter III
MIGRATION

The migrants

The migration of animals has always attracted attention, but generally two quite distinct phenomena are confused under this term. Groups may at various times leave the areas they inhabit, usually without hope of return, such as the migrations of lemmings in the Arctic, locusts in Africa, etc. Very different are other movements which are distinguished by periodic changes of habitation of individuals, occurring at fixed dates, between determined zones. It is to this definition of the term that the migrations of birds chiefly refer. Migrations of the first type, which also occur in birds, are preferably termed invasions or irruptions; further there are intermediate stages between the two phenomena.

Formerly, birds were classified as either erratic, sedentary, or migrants, but this far too simple division hardly meets the case. True sedentary birds are rare,

and all stages exist between them and real migrants such as Swallows. Everyone has seen the great gatherings of these birds in autumn, their preparatory flights, and the sudden departure of the whole flock; European Swallows travel as far as South Africa; they do not return for six months, and then in less compact flocks than those in which they leave. The majority of small insectivorous birds do the same, but the nocturnal departure of birds which have stopped singing for some time is not noticed in the same way.

Others do not leave so suddenly. A varying number of Blackcaps and Black Redstarts, which even sing in autumn, remains till the onset of winter, and some spend the winter in southern France; the return in spring is also gradual, their migration, although on the whole distinct, being no longer a well-marked phenomenon. Some individual Chiffchaffs may winter in the south of England, but others may reach southern Africa. On other occasions a species which is present all the year round is really migratory, because local

individuals are replaced by birds coming from colder regions; the "centre of gravity" of the species is moved. Also migrations are often only observed in one part of the total area of distribution, the individuals inhabiting places with mild winters making only limited local movements; these individuals may differ morphologically by having slightly shorter wings.

Finally, some birds make quite considerable irregular movements in accordance with the prevailing climatic conditions. It is a movement more like that of herds of cattle changing to and from alpine pastures than true migration.

In Europe the only true sedentary birds are the gallinaceous birds (except the Quail), certain Owls, Woodpeckers, and some Corvidae. At different dates, varying according to the species, there is merely a more or less wide dispersal of the young birds, but the adults may pass their entire lives in a clearly defined area. It is curious that Ptarmigan, which are among the most sedentary of birds, have a particularly inhospitable habitat in winter—arctic

Flight of White-fronted Geese wintering in western Flanders.

149

Migratory flight of Oystercatchers.

valley of the Mississippi and Central America; the adults go south straight across the Atlantic by way of Bermuda, and all return by the land route in spring.

When sexual maturity is not developed for several years the young birds may wait to attain this before returning; for instance Storks do not return until they are three, and Egyptian Vultures until they are seven years old.

Some species are distributed over widely different latitudes, and consequently widely different climates. In this case, races inhabiting cold regions frequently migrate before those of temperate zones and pass over them during their autumn migration, arriving at their winter quarters; in spring they stay behind longer and the same phenomenon occurs in the reverse way.

Generally late migrants have their post-nuptial moult before departure; those which leave early moult after arriving at their winter quarters (Swifts, Cuckoos). Some stop to moult during their journey, and it is for this reason that the Lapwings of North and North-West Europe concentrate in Belgium and Holland; some northern Ducks spend several weeks in the region of the Caspian and on certain Himalayan lakes,

regions and high mountains— where it seems difficult to believe a bird would be found at that time and where they remain practically alone.

Specific variations in the migratory instinct are complicated by individual variations. As a general rule when migration is not total, the males move less than the females and young, but often quite irregularly, and an individual may migrate one year but not the next, and conversely. Thus in temperate Europe the winter populations of Robins contain a majority of males, while in the plains of Algeria females almost exclusively are found; in the mountains of North Africa the local sedentary race shows no shift of sex ratio. In the same way, adult males are very rare in the flocks of northern Ducks which appear in France during the greatest cold. One

example will show how individual variation can be very important; of two young Blackbirds of the same brood born at Frankfurt-on-Main, in the following winter one was found at its place of birth and the other in south-western France.

Even when all the individuals of a species migrate, the methods of departure of the young may differ from that of the adults. The adults often leave first, in Cuckoos even as much as six weeks ahead. In the Lapwing, on the contrary, the young go first. Before the final departure, the birds of the year may disperse in such a way that they sometimes take the opposite direction to that of their main journey. Some birds do not follow the same migration routes as their parents—the young of the American Golden Plover born in the Arctic migrate to South America through Canada, the

Sand-Martins (Bank Swallows). A flock at rest on migration.

before reaching their winter quarters.

Movements are made by day or by night according to the species. Many small otherwise diurnal Passerines, especially those that are insectivorous, travel at night and spend the day feeding. Some birds, diurnal birds of prey among others, may travel singly, but most other day-migrants move in flocks. Small birds form into more or less compact groups whose composition is constantly changing; certain large birds have regular formations, and the transverse lines of Cranes and the triangular formations of Ducks and Geese are famous.

Penguins, being unable to fly, migrate by swimming. Guillemots also do this regularly, and Geese have been observed swimming between seven and eight miles a day.

The speeds at which these migratory movements are made differ very little from those of ordinary flights, i.e. 19–25 m.p.h. for small birds. The altitude for which radar observations enable fairly exact calculations to be made, both by day and by night, varies considerably. While certain species travel fairly close to the ground or near the surface of the sea, many fly at a height of between

3,000 and 4,700 ft.; some have even been detected at 22,000 ft. These altitudes are subject to variations according to prevailing circumstances. Passerines have a tendency to fly at a greater height on their return in the spring than on their departure in the autumn, and also higher at night than by day.

The daily duration of flight seems generally to be from six to eight hours, although when crossing regions which offer little opportunity for resting the flights may be of much longer duration. It has been estimated that the crossing of the Gulf of Mexico may take from 24 to 36 hours, and the Sahara up to 60 hours.

In the great majority of cases adult birds return to the nesting places of the previous year. Sometimes in the Anatidae one mate follows the other into an area far away from its own birth-place. The Short-eared Owl, like a few other species, does not return to any fixed locality; it nests where small rodents are abundant and it is well known how the numbers of these mammals may vary from year to year.

During the course of migration, for various reasons which are generally very difficult to define, birds are sometimes deflected from their routes and appear in unexpected places. Big storms are often responsible and several authentic cases are known, such as Lapwings crossing the Atlantic from Ireland to Newfoundland in 24 hours. In January 1937 Fieldfares blown by a south-easterly wind crossed the North Atlantic and reached Greenland, which they also crossed a few days later, and finally settled on the southwest coast. Since then they have nested there and it is remarkable that they have lost their migratory habits.

Flight of Brent Geese.

Geography of migrations

When the directions followed by birds are examined, the question arises as to whether in a general way they travel on well defined routes or spread out on a wide front with no particular concentrations. The problem has long been discussed but, as publications accumulate, it must be admitted that each of these explanations is incomplete.

Small birds in more or less compact groups usually travel on a wide front, but owing to their relatively poor power of flight they prefer to go round obstacles rather than fly over them; therefore concentrations are observed in certain places which makes it possible to believe in narrow routes. The phenomenon is marked along the coasts; 'flocks of Passerines arriving in sight of the sea change direction, and follow the shore and do not cross over the sea till they reach a promontory which forms a kind of jumping-off place; at sea, islands are concentration points which stand out as landmarks on the routes. It must be noted, however, that they are not indispensable, as birds, even apparently poor flyers, traverse vast expanses of the ocean: for instance, Humming Birds are said to travel regularly from Chile to the Juan

Fernandez Islands, about 450 miles, without any possibility of alighting en route.

High mountains may alter the route of birds of weaker flight, who either go round them, or follow the valleys which lead to more accessible passes. A change in the nature of the region traversed may modify the routes of species which show a preference for certain types of terrain, and, for example, concentrations of migrants are seen skirting forests without penetrating them. The feeding possibilities are also a consideration — deserts which, like the ocean, do not usually constitute an insurmountable obstacle, since oases constitute resting and feeding places, are avoided by the majority of wading birds which prefer to keep to the coast.

These various factors are not sufficient to account for all the routes, and specific elements may be superimposed. Thus of two allied species which nest together in the East Siberian Arctic, the Siberian Pectoral Sandpiper and the American Pectoral Sandpiper, whereas the first goes south along the coast of Asia the second goes east, to join its North American relatives, and winters with them in South America. The west to east flight apparently

The Rufous Humming Bird (here shown life-size), the most northerly of all Humming Birds, breeds as far north as south-east Alaska and winters in southern Mexico. Others in its family are migratory, but none travel so far.

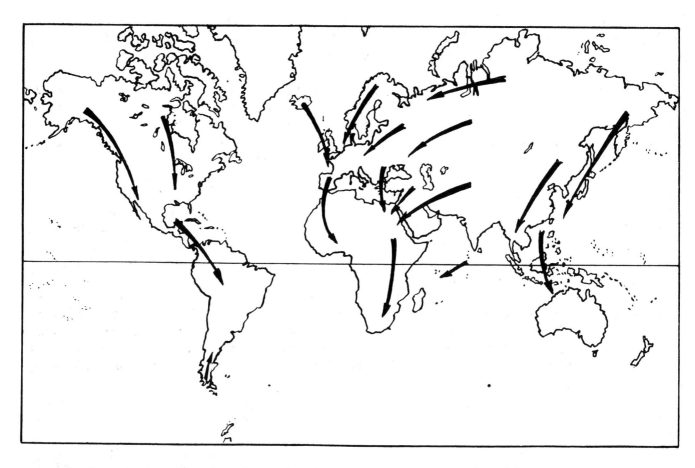

corresponds to an ancient immigration route.

A general rule can be laid down that the more severe the winter is in a region the larger the number of migrants among the birds which are found there, and though there are migrants in all climates there are the greatest number in cold and temperate countries.

In Northern Europe, populated as far as latitude 80° N at Spitzbergen, almost the entire avian population leaves in winter. In temperate Europe it is mostly the insectivorous birds which migrate, and even in the Mediterranean region a large number leave for the south in autumn.

The amount of migration increases from south-west to northeast of Europe both in the number of different species and the number of individuals of each species. Sedentary birds such as the Magpie and the Partridge show migratory tendencies in the extreme north-east of their range; on the other hand, in Western Europe the mild climate makes it possible for many birds with omnivorous feeding habits to remain, or merely move a short distance, not passing further south than the Mediterranean.

The whole movement of autumn departure which is almost

General diagram of the principal migration routes.

in the direction of west to east in West Siberia becomes north-east to south-west in Scandinavia and Central Europe, and markedly north to south only in the most westerly regions.

Thus a very large number of northern birds, chiefly the Limicolae, such as Godwits, Sandpipers, etc., pass along the Atlantic coasts to France in particular, and follow the sea-shore on account of the abundant food which they find there. From Scandinavia they reach the North Sea and the coasts of England, then those of the

English Channel and join up with the birds which, travelling from Iceland by way of the Faeroe Islands, have reached the coasts of Scotland and Ireland, where their numbers are greatly increased by local birds. With them are birds which have come from still more distant places such as, among land birds, the Greenland Wheatear which winters in West Africa where it was originally discovered and was therefore given the name of Senegal Wheatear by the older authors.

It is not only land birds which travel inland; numbers of aquatic birds also follow the large waterways as is evidenced among other examples by the fact that Divers [Loons], Cormorants, Scoters, Long-tailed Ducks [Old Squaws] and many other water birds are observed regularly on the Swiss Lakes.

In the interior of France flights of Cranes and Storks come in autumn from north-eastern Europe. Rooks which winter in France, Spain and Portugal arrive from Germany, Poland, the Baltic countries and Russia, and though schematically this great north-east to south-west movement, with its numerous variations of detail, gives a reasonably good picture of migration in Europe, all the routes should be taken into consideration. There are notable exceptions, the most striking perhaps being that of the Red-breasted Flycatcher which nests in Central and Eastern Europe and winters in India. The Golden Orioles also take a south-eastern

direction; starting in August, they fly through Italy and the Balkans, then gather in the plains of Greece, which they leave in September for East Africa. However, the return journey is quite different; they reach Europe after having crossed the Sahara in a north-westerly direction and then the whole breadth of the Mediterranean.

There are two principal routes for the birds which leave Europe for Africa: some by way of Spain or Italy reach first North and then West Africa; others travelling via the Balkans and East Mediterranean go to the east and south of the continent by the valley of the Nile. However, the

Sahara is in no way an insurmountable barrier, but like the oceans it is traversed at greater speed than the rest of the distance covered, and though the concentration is greater at each end, it can be said that a more or less dense wave traverses it along the whole breadth of Africa.

Mediterranean Africa serves as a wintering-place for a certain number of European species, such as the Starling, Blackcap, Song-Thrush, etc. The majority of insectivorous birds reach tropical and even southern Africa. Swallows which have nested in Europe winter from October to March partly in the extreme south but chiefly in the equatorial zone;

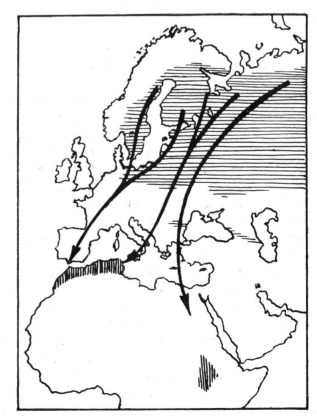

Migration of the European Common Crane: horizontal hatching indicates breeding areas, vertical hatching indicates winter-quarters.

Migratory flocks may comprise several species of birds. It is common to see, as here, large mixed flights of Dunlin and Ringed Plover.

European Roller photographed during its winter stay in East Africa.

The large flat expanses in Friesland count among the favourite winter-quarters of flocks of Grey Lag Geese which have come from the north.

Eastern White Pelicans displaying as one of their own species arrives at the colony.

Flamingos are among the most gregarious of birds. In the nesting colonies the nests are extremely close together.

A flock of Eastern White Pelicans. East Africa.

some therefore cover a distance of almost 6,250 miles in each direction. Although this bird is one about which there is the most information, because of the large number that have been ringed, it is difficult to define its winter range on account of its erratic behaviour at this season, and also because of the absence of data from many of the less frequented regions. The House-Martin, which comes from the same localities, seems to be localised in the two zones corresponding to the two principal streams, on the one hand West Africa north of the equator, and on the other hand the east and south.

Aquatic birds travel along the coast, but when favourable regions are reached, some species, following the rivers, penetrate far into the interior and, especially in lacustrine regions, there is an abundance of small northern waders in winter. Sandpipers are chiefly met with, as many species do not leave the coast; the Sanderling, which nests in the high latitudes of the Arctic such as Greenland, Spitzbergen, Taimyr Peninsula, etc., is found as far south as the Cape; in the same way the American populations of this species go as far as Patagonia; and those of East Siberia to Australia.

If Africa, especially the eastern part, constitutes the wintering quarters of a large number of European birds they are not the only ones that abound; there are, for instance, quite as many mi-grants from Eastern, Central and Northern Asia, and even India. Like the majority of their European relatives, these birds follow a general north-easterly to south-westerly direction and, crossing Persia, Arabia and the Red Sea, they reach the valley of the Nile. The east to west tendency can be quite accentuated, as for example the Slender-billed Curlew, which nests in Siberia in the region of the Irtysh, spends the winter on the European coasts of the Mediterranean. The Isabelline Shrike of Central Asia goes to Chari to finish its autumn moult, and during the first months of the year the Demoiselle Crane, which nests in the region of the Caspian and Central Asia, goes in large numbers to Lake Tchad and to the Sudan.

In spite of its relative isolation, a large quantity of birds migrate to Madagascar as much from Europe and Western Asia as from Eastern Asia. They are chiefly good flyers, such as Curlews, Plovers and Sandpipers, but also birds with less sustained flight, such as the Corncrake.

Not all the migrants of Central Asia travel to Africa; some, such as the Bar-headed Goose, go south and, crossing the chain of the Himalayas, winter in India. In the Himalayas themselves there is little movement, the birds finding easy conditions in the lower regions during the winter. But nevertheless some cases of quite distinct migration occur; the Woodcock and a species of Night-ingale winter in the mountains in the extreme south of India, the Indian Orange-headed Ground-Thrush migrates to the plains as far south as Ceylon, and the local race of the Swallow as far as Burma.

In the Far East the migratory movement is extremely accentuated. The hardness of the winter, as well as the shorter distance from the equator, cause the departure of a much larger number of species than in Europe; in the neighbourhood of the tropics the seed-eating Passerines, which undertake long winter journeys, are again numerous. This tendency is accentuated by the fact that a large number of the species are of tropical origin; there is actually no natural barrier which could have impeded the dispersion of species northwards as the Sahara — and, to a lesser degree, the Mediterranean—have done in Europe for the African birds. Therefore a much larger migratory stream than that in Europe proceeds towards the south, comprising birds of Siberia, Mongolia, Japan and North China. By way of Indo-China and the Philippines they reach the Malay Archipelago, some push on as far as the Australian region, and others turn west towards Madagascar.

In the north of the New World the situation is somewhat similar to that of the Far East, no important obstacle stopping the spread of southern species; Tanagers and Humming Birds nest in Canada, one of them even in Alaska. The migration spreads across the

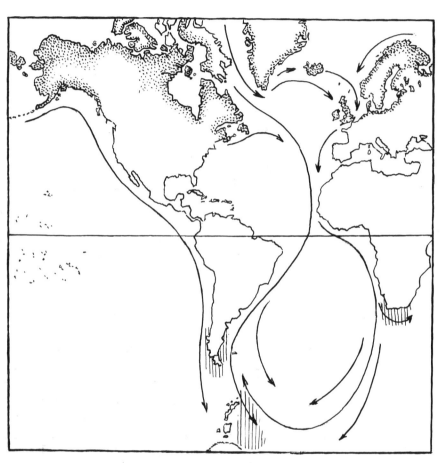

hemisphere, they are on the whole of very reduced amplitude. East of the Andes the migrants do not go further north than the province of Buenos Aires, but on the west side, which is cooled by the Humboldt current, they go as far as Peru. Only very few species, notably Swallows, cross the Equator.

In New Zealand, a very few species, including a single Passerine, migrate from South Island to North Island, and except for a Pigeon, which winters in Australia, the only long migrations are made by two Cuckoos: the Long-tailed Cuckoo of "Tahiti" leaves for the north-north-east to pass the winter in the South Sea archipelagos from Fiji to the Society Islands and the Broadbilled Bronze Cuckoo for the north-north-west to the Bismarck and Solomon Islands. In Southern Australia there are remarkably few migrant birds, though some Cuckoos, a Bee-eater, a Kingfisher, and some others, winter further north, occasionally as far as Malaya.

Although they do not have the same seasonal changes as temperate countries, tropical regions are none the less the site of migrations, sometimes of considerable magnitude. They are not very well-known and further it is difficult to distinguish clearly between true migration and more or less accentuated erratic movements

whole breadth of the continent. It is, however, denser on the natural routes formed by the Pacific and Atlantic coasts, the Rocky Mountains and the basin of the Mississippi. Some stop in the south of the United States, others in Mexico, but still more go by Central America, populating the north-west of the South American continent after having crossed the Andes of Colombia; some land species even reach the Argentine, and shore birds Patagonia.

Land migration is much less in the southern hemisphere, for the simple reason that, owing to the very reduced size of the continents, much less movement is possible. At the latitude of the centre of France, the 47th Parallel passes through America, Europe and Asia, traversing a land surface amounting to 205° of the earth's circumference, while the corresponding latitude in the south only crosses Stewart Island, the extreme limit of New Zealand territory, and the South American continent comprising only 8°. It is in the South American continent that the migratory movements are most generalised but, unlike those of the northern

Pair of Arctic Terns.

resulting only from variation in local conditions. But actually quite a large number of well-defined cases are known.

In tropical Africa the existence of regularly alternating dry and rainy seasons determines the movements of a certain number of insectivorous birds. The Pennant-wing Nightjar, which breeds from September to November during the rainy season in the South African veldt, traverses the equatorial forests to pass the months of April to July in the Sudan savannas where it arrives to find a further rainy season.

A Roller from Madagascar goes for several months to the African continent as far as the north of the Kinshasa region of the Congo, and conversely, the Sooty Falcon, which nests in north-east Africa, spends November to April in Madagascar.

Cases of migration are known between India and East Africa, and between North Australia and the Bismarck and Solomon Islands. There are also similar examples in tropical America, but they are probably less numerous; we will only mention the two Vireos, one of which travels between Cuba and Colombia, and the other between the tropical zone of Mexico and the upper Amazon.

The migrations of marine species are no less important than those of land birds and, like them, are not restricted to areas where

the rigours of the winter climate compel them to move away in order to get sufficient food. Shearwaters which nest in Australian waters make particularly long journeys, taking them during the northern summer to arctic regions where analogous species, which move to a far lesser degree, are nesting at this time. The Great Shearwater, which nests in the Islands of Tristan da Cunha, goes up the western zone of the Atlantic Ocean to Greenland, then comes down again along the coasts of Europe, returning to its nesting place by way of various islands in the Atlantic. A round journey of similar extent, but of still greater amplitude, is made by the Short-tailed Shearwater, which nests in the islets off the coasts of New Zealand and South Australia and goes via the islands of Melanesia, along the archipelago of Eastern Asia to the ex-

treme north of the Pacific, sometimes even passing the Behring Straits, and having followed the American coasts towards Lower California, crosses the Pacific diagonally to rejoin the Australian waters, accomplishing each year a circuit of at least 18,750 miles.

If in the northern hemisphere the Procellariiformes travel less than their relatives in the south, nevertheless extensive movements have been observed in other groups. The Arctic Tern winters on the coasts of the southern hemisphere and has even been found in the pack ice at latitude 64° S; the Turnstone goes as far as New Zealand and Chile; and the Bristle-thighed or Tahitian Curlew, so named after its winter quarters in the Polynesian islands, nests only in Alaska. Its sea voyage, without any possibility of landing, is one of the longest known.

Problems of migration

The various aspects of migration behaviour raise numerous questions altogether different from the simple problem which long divided naturalists as to whether migration existed or not. The most extravagant hypotheses were propounded to explain the disappearance of birds in winter, such as submergence in ponds or even travelling to the moon; the most rational was that birds hibernated, and there were still supporters of this theory at the beginning of the 19th century. It is curious that not until the middle of the 20th century was it established that birds actually do hibernate, at least in the case of one species, the Poorwill.

It is conceivable that there is some connection between migration and availability of food. Yet another example of the wide range of different aspects of the phenomenon is shown in the populations of the Courser and Rufous-tailed Finch Lark of the extreme south of Morocco, which, after having nested at the beginning of the year, migrate northwards, thus avoiding the heat of the Saharan summer.

Nevertheless, when an attempt is made to define accurately the connection between migrations and local conditions it is found that this is not simple and in particular that migrants leave before the situation has become unfavourable. It has already been mentioned that adult Cuckoos precede the young by several weeks, and nevertheless the young birds are always able to find means of subsistence. Swifts leave us in high summer, when insects are plentiful, whereas Alpine Swifts, which inhabit mountains, where food must be much scarcer, remain much longer. This is attributable to the fact that migrants leave with considerable reserves of fat which could not be formed without a superabundant diet.

Meteorological factors influence migration; the effects of temperature, pressure, wind, the amount of electricity in the atmosphere, etc., have all been studied. Although the results obtained are interesting, no generalisation can be made, since, as in everything concerning migration, there are considerable specific and local variations.

What appears to influence migration is meteorological condi-

Grey Lag Geese migrating. Migrants such as Ducks, Geese, Storks, Cranes, often fly in lines or V formations.

tions taken as a whole, these conditions recurring in a more or less identical manner every year.

The arrival in Europe in spring of certain birds like the Swallow follows more or less regularly the advance of isotherms, but there is no correlation in other species, such as the Red-backed Shrike. In the northern hemisphere there is generally an intensification of migratory movements between a rise and fall in temperature at this season; sudden severe cold causes some species to return but does not affect others.

Though external factors affect the actual migration, it is the internal condition of the bird which fundamentally induces migratory activity; migration, like reproduction, is a phase of the annual physiological cycle the mechanism of which is not yet quite clear. It should be emphasised that castrated birds migrate; the phenomenon seems to be directly dominated by the pituitary and not by the condition of the gonads or the thyroid.

The great problem raised by migration is that of orientation; how does a bird find its way over a distance often of thousands of miles?

The Carrier Pigeon, although not a migrant, raises a very similar problem. Numerous studies have shown that it uses visual cues. During fog, or on a dark night, or if it is released at sea, the bird returns very late or may even get lost. Over a distance it knows, the speed is greater.

Nevertheless, there are also cases of the rapid return of individuals released in unfamiliar places a great distance away from the nest. This ability to return home is not confined to Pigeons, and there are records of birds liberated outside their normal range returning to the nest. The Manx Shearwaters of the coasts of Cornwall, which normally never pass beyond the Irish Sea and the Bay of Biscay, have returned to the nest after having been released at Boston (U.S.A.), the Faeroe Islands, Venice, and even in Switzerland, far from the sea.

Although returning to the nest is a different phenomenon to that of migration, it must be admitted that the bird is capable of finding its way without any known landmarks; young birds making their first migration alone furnish yet another proof.

Could one speak of a "sense of direction", as has been suggested? This could only be a gratuitous proposition since its anatomical basis is not known. Various

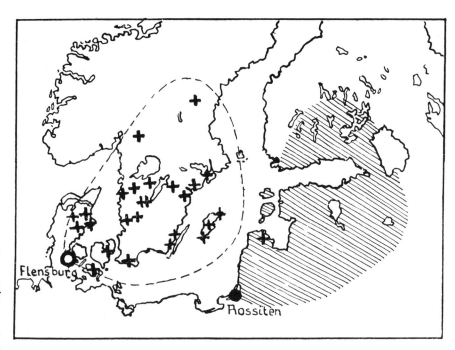

hypotheses have been put forward, including those which relate this direction-finding faculty to the perception of earth magnetism or to that of Corioli's force, produced by the rotation of the earth and which varies with latitude. It seems that none of these hypotheses can be sustained.

A number of far-reaching experiments carried out, especially during the last few years, have led to some new concepts of this "sense".

To begin with, it was observed that migrants did not take a route to a specific place but in a specific direction. This is why birds that have deviated from their course during their spring migration (see map above) have followed a course parallel to the one they would normally have taken.

Some birds kept in captivity assemble, at the time of migration, in the part of the cage corresponding to the direction which they would normally take. If the light which they receive from the sky is deflected at an angle by mirrors, they take a direction deflected at the same angle in relation to their normal direction. If the sky is very overcast they disperse haphazardly. In an enclosed space an artificial sun yields the same results.

The inference is that orientation of diurnal migrants is made with the aid of the sun's rays. Nocturnal migrants take their direction from the stars, as suggested by experiments carried out in a planetarium with the image of the constellations.

It must be noted that in these conditions the bird knows instinctively at any given moment the angle which its route must make with the position of the stars — an angle which varies throughout the daily cycle. This implies an appreciation, albeit unconscious, of what we call exact time; everything happens as if the bird itself could be assimilated to a clock. Some captive migrants, having no other visual guide than a motionless artificial sun, progressively change their direction by reference to this sun as they would do in full daylight.

If these facts enable us to understand fairly well the orientation of migrants during their journeys, they do not suffice to explain the return of birds which have gone off course. With migrants everything happens as if they knew in advance the direction they must take, whereas the bird which is released in a random place cannot know its direction and must determine it at the moment it is released according to the position of that place, wherever situated.

It would seem that instinctively the bird "takes its bearings" just as navigators do by referring to the position of the sun. In its apparent movement the sun passes to its highest point—at midday, solar time, for us—at precisely the same moment in all places which have the same longitude. This maximal height above the horizon is the same for all places of the same latitude but varies with the time of year. A bird knowing the characteristics of solar movement in the place where it normally lives would compare them with those in the place where it finds itself and so would infer the direction to follow. This explanation is, of course, expressed in anthropomorphic terms since it is impossible for us to know what the creature really feels.

Nor can this be regarded as any more than a hypothesis. It may seem impossible because of the precise details which it implies, particularly in the appreciation of time, a detail all the more extraordinary in that the position of the sun at midday must be able to be estimated from what the bird perceives at any given moment of the day.

Experiments have, however, shown that such precise details in the perception of the outside world are possible with birds. Their daily and annual rhythms may follow a schedule rigorous enough for us to observe the fact, quoted above, of the laying of a single egg on precisely the same date every year. None of this is fundamentally more extraordinary than the precision of a dog's sense of smell, which does not surprise us despite the fact that our own sense of smell is in no way comparable.

The interest aroused by the phenomenon of the migration of birds has always been so great that particular attention has been paid, more perhaps than to any other aspect of their behaviour, to seeking its origin.

It is generally admitted that the birds of temperate regions, driven from their habitat by the extension of glaciers in the pleistocene age, and then, after the moderating of the climate, re-taking possession of their ancient territories, acquired by natural selection the instinct to return to spend the summer in the countries from which they had been forced away.

Nevertheless, propounded in this way, this very plausible hypothesis is much too limited in character. Migration exists in birds whose habitats have never been touched by the quaternary glaciation. Furthermore it would be very extraordinary for birds of far more remote geological times, with the osteological characteristics of existing species, and therefore almost certainly their same abilities of movement, to have waited for the glacial age to develop instincts of this kind. Migrations of one type or another must have appeared at all times as adaptations to climatic variations, and the modifications of quaternary glaciers could only have influenced the actual manifestations of migration in temperate regions. Nor does this hypothesis take into account the necessity for very long migrations, the full extent of which is to be related to the fact that birds can only stay where they can find an adequate food supply, that is to say in places where the totality of the resources is not utilised by the local species. The tropical savannas, in particular, subject as they are to clearly defined alternate seasons of dryness and humidity, are a case in point. The incumbents whose resources are limited by the unfavourable conditions of the dry season could not possibly exhaust the resources of the wet season. Migrants profit from this, which explains their abundance in these places.

It should be noted that during the summer these same migrants find themselves in an analogous situation in regard to the incumbents of the regions where they nest.

The study of migration has long had to content itself with direct observations during passage and the collation of places of origin of specimens in collections, but it has been greatly facilitated by the "ringing" or "banding" of birds. As is well known this method consists in catching a bird and then releasing it after having affixed to its leg an aluminium ring bearing a serial number and the name of the ringing scheme under which it is operated. By means of the recoveries of ringed birds found dead, killed by sportsmen, or captured for this purpose, the routes are determined.

Rings can easily be placed on nestlings while still in the nest. At ornithological stations traps are constructed by means of which large numbers of birds are caught and ringed on passage.

Rings have the disadvantage that the capture of the subject is

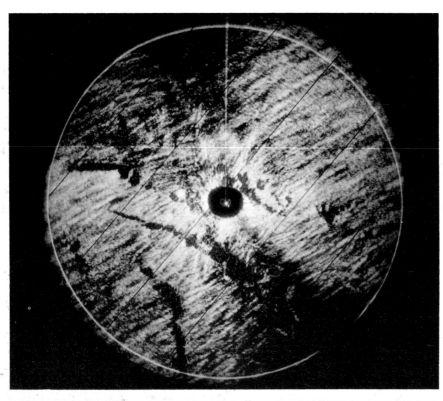

Autumn migration observed at night on a radar screen at Zurich-Kloten airport.
The vertical white line indicates North; the white circle delimits a zone 22½ miles in diameter the centre of which is the radar. The dark zones correspond to hilly regions.
Top (exposure time: 2 minutes): normal regular stream of migrants making their way southwestwards.
Below (exposure time: 4 minutes): a strong westerly wind blows the birds off course in a southerly direction; some are even being swept away to the east.

necessary in order to obtain any useful information. To amplify their use, the visible parts of the plumage of birds have been dyed. But this method, by which it is possible to follow the movements of marked birds without capturing them, can only be used to a limited extent because of its very transitory character.

For a number of years radar has been providing information previously impossible to obtain. Migratory flights are tracked over great distances—more than 60 miles each day and each night—across seas as well as over land. The size of all the migratory flights put together can be assessed, and the altitude of the flights can be measured; unfortunately the identification of species is beyond the power of radar.

By attaching miniaturised transmitters to birds it is possible to follow their course by the classic methods of radiolocation, and this procedure has also been of practical use in research.

Outside the breeding season, flocks of Flamingos can number thousands, like this flock of Lesser Flamingos on Lake Magadi in Kenya. ▶

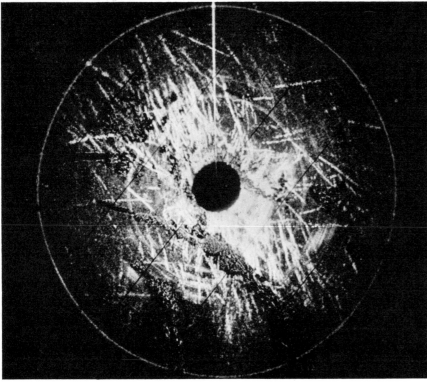

166

*In certain circumstances gregarious ten-
dencies can bring together different species
of similar habits, as may be seen in this
photograph of a nesting colony of Sacred
Ibises and several species of Herons.*

Colony of Weavers. East Africa.

Chapter IV
SOLITARY AND GREGARIOUS BIRDS

Individuals of the same species of birds almost invariably show a tendency, at one time or another during their life, to form into groups; except for certain sedentary birds, very few lead a consistently solitary existence outside the breeding season. Diurnal and nocturnal birds of prey, among others, are rare examples. On the other hand, there are but few instances of permanent associations, and between the two extremes there is a great variety of diverse, and more or less temporary, groupings. Knowledge of this complex subject is still so incomplete, especially concerning tropical species, and the diversity of known associations so great, as to make any generalisation imprudent at the present time.

Exceptional circumstances may cause birds which are normally solitary to form into groups. In the winter months birds frequently assemble together at night to shelter from bad weather, and as many as thirty Wrens have been found sleeping together in House-Martins' nests. As a result of an unusual abundance of food, temporary assemblies may be formed in which each bird seeks a purely individual advantage without any real social inclinations; on the contrary there is often competition between individuals, as in the well known case of Vultures gathered round a carcase.

Many small Passerines which

Puffins, which nest in burrows, gather together in their idle moments.

169

Emperor Penguins. Young birds congregate in "nurseries". The adults which crowd round to shelter them from a blizzard cannot, however, prevent them from being partly covered by ice.

have very marked territorial behaviour in the breeding season tend to be gregarious at other times. These winter bands show little organisation and their composition is constantly changing. Often several different species congregate together in this way; the mixed flocks of Fringillidae, Chaffinches, Buntings, etc., are well known, as also are those of Rooks and Jackdaws, Icteridae, "Blackbirds" in America, with which Starlings often mingle. Bands of Tits, which are slightly different in character because of their continual wanderings into the forest, are frequently accompanied by Nuthatches, Treecreepers, and even Woodpeckers, though those birds obtain their food in a different way. Such itinerant assemblies are common at all times of the year in tropical forests and are composed of widely different species.

Though birds which are normally gregarious usually separate during the breeding season, the opposite also occurs, such as, among others, the assemblies of Grouse for their communal displays. It is stated that in the Sage Grouse a temporary hierarchy is established between the cocks on which depends their relations with the hens; those of the highest "rank" securing the favours of most females. Some Albatrosses, which lead a wandering life over the oceans throughout the year, assemble together to nest. Often species with gregarious tendencies, but normally without specific organisation, show a much more clearly marked social behaviour during the nesting season. Generally there is merely a collection of individual nests on a limited area, the immediate surroundings of which are defended by the pair; this is the case in many sea-

birds such as Gulls, Terns, etc., as well as Weavers, Herons and many other birds. Sometimes, as in the case of the Black-headed Gull, many nests are built close together, forming a great colony of small groups in which the social bond is strengthened. Gregariousness may continue outside the colony, and the birds remain in groups to search for food; there may even be concerted action such as the collective fishing by certain Cormorants in which different species from neighbouring colonies sometimes take part, such as Shags, Razorbills, Guillemots and Puffins on the coasts of the Atlantic. This attraction between different species of birds may occur without apparent material advantage; for instance Guillemots may be seen spending some time in colonies of Shags whose company they seem to appreciate.

Oystercatchers. When migrating, birds which are usually solitary may show strong gregarious tendencies. Flocks exhibit a striking unity of movement and when at rest individual birds often assume the same attitude. ▶

Social organisation may be developed to such a degree that some phases of nest-building may be carried out communally. Among land-birds the Anis of tropical America exemplify this; these Cuckoos show considerable specific and individual differences in this behaviour. There may be isolated nests, but most frequently several pairs defend a common territory and build a single nest in which all the eggs are laid; and polygamy even occurs at times. All the members of the community share in incubating the eggs and bringing up the young birds.

In some Penguins, Flamingos, and the Sandwich Tern, each pair builds a nest and incubates its eggs but, sooner or later, the young birds gather together and form nurseries attended by a few adults. In the Emperor Penguins the eggs are incubated indiscriminately by all the adults, even by non-breeding birds, and the young are assembled together in nurseries. To what extent the parents recognise and feed only their own young is still disputed.

Though in most gregarious Weavers the nests are merely placed near each other without any close ties existing between the builders, the South African Sociable Weaverbirds construct a vast edifice in which the nests are placed side by side under a common roof built by all the members of the community before they start on their own nests.

In the cases just mentioned the community shows definite organisation only during the nesting

Nesting colony of Great Cormorants.

172

season, but there are groupings where social conduct is governed by strict laws at all times; colonies of this type are found in particular in the Corvidae where they have been carefully studied. Thus, in Jackdaws each pair has its own nest, but all birds join in defending a common territory. Each is individually known to the others, and outsiders are admitted only in autumn and winter. If a member of the community is attacked, whether by a predator, or by one of its fellows in the course of a quarrel, the others immediately open attack on the assailant. There is a well-defined hierarchy in the colony, but domination is chiefly exercised between birds of fairly equal status, those at the bottom of the scale being tolerated by those of highest rank. Young female birds, which almost invariably rank very low, assume the rank of their mate when paired.

This social hierarchy under which certain individuals have some sort of right of precedence over others in the various activities of communal life, especially with regard to food, is fairly common in bird communities.

Nests of the Sociable Weaverbird. South Africa. Individual nests are crowded under one roof which is built communally beforehand by all members of the colony.

The ecstatic display of the Adélie Penguin. In this attitude, which is assumed by single birds but is sometimes contagious, the body is held rigid and motionless, the wings beat slowly and peculiar sounds are uttered. The significance of this display is obscure.

Emperor Penguin rookery at Adélie Land. While the chicks are still small they are brooded individually by the adults. ▶

King Penguin rookery. South Georgia. The birds in the foreground are brooding; the egg is placed on the feet and covered with a fold of skin from the ventral surface. Each bird seems to regulate its position by that of its neighbour, resulting in the formation of almost straight lines.

instantaneously followed by others, who are already disposed to act in the same way; this assures an almost absolute simultaneity of movement.

It is common, especially in nesting colonies of certain species, for the birds to take flight suddenly and simultaneously, often for no apparent reason. The abrupt departure of one individual is a signal which automatically starts off all the others, and frequently the conspicuous parts of the plumage which are hidden whilst the bird is at rest are suddenly displayed on its taking flight, changing its appearance and accentuating the movement. These contagious panics might well be disastrous in the long run, so in many cases there are some attitudes with a special significance, a sort of intention movement which announces the intention of the performer and prevents its example being followed unnecessarily.

This type of contagious behaviour occurs in a great variety of circumstances. If a domestic fowl, kept apart from its fellows, is offered food until it is crammed full and refuses to eat any more, it nevertheless starts feeding again if put back in the yard where the others are being fed. If in a group of Guillemots or Rock-Doves a

This has not been studied to any great extent except in captive or domestic birds, where these manifestations seem to be of much greater importance than in birds of the wild. Hence in many cases it is still difficult to determine the consequences of this domination.

It may be asked to what extent gregarious birds benefit from their social behaviour. To understand the mode of life of gregarious birds both the psychological and physiological influences which individuals reciprocally exercise on each other should first be taken into consideration.

As always in such cases these influences are subtle, vary with the species, and are sometimes very difficult to define exactly, though certain phenomena are nevertheless very clear.

The co-ordination of movements in some flocks of birds is well known. Anyone can observe the unanimity of movement with which the individual birds in a flight of Starlings or Sandpipers carry out their evolutions. It seems as though there is a collective reaction to the same influences, and that the movements of those which take the lead are

Nesting colony of Dalmatian Pelicans.

177

pair abandon their eggs others often follow suit.

In a colony of sea-birds the cry of one individual may be enough to set the others off and may even end in neighbouring colonies joining in the concert; similarly when a pair begins to display, others display also, to such a degree that it is difficult to determine the significance of certain ritual gestures which might quite as well be an expression of social ties as a manifestation of sexual behaviour. This state of things results in a synchronisation of reproductive activity inside a colony, and consequently a reduction of the time during which eggs or defenceless chicks are collected together, thereby reducing the chances of destruction.

These reciprocal influences are clearly evidenced by an experiment carried out on Bob White Partridges. By the injection of hormones, several pairs were made to breed before their normal time, and several other pairs living with them, which were not injected, also bred much earlier than usual. The stimulus given by the behaviour of the birds injected with hormones was sufficient to activate the physiological condition of the others. Breeders of Budgerigars know that their birds breed better when several pairs are kept in one aviary, differing from birds with territorial behaviour, such as Chaffinches, or European Robins, in which only a single pair will breed when several are kept in one cage.

Gregarious birds therefore seem to have a characteristic tendency to assume the same psychological and physiological condition as the other members of their community. Certain collective manifestations may be of a somewhat different character. Thus a cry of alarm from a bird in danger may in some cases release a general demonstration of hostility against the aggressor; and here the individual instinctive reaction differs from the action which stimulates it; the first bird cries out, the others attack, and this reaction is so automatic that the aggressor itself, if a member of the community, may join in the display of hostility; which in effect causes the aggression to cease.

To sum up, it may be said that it is necessary for some species to live in communities, just as, for example, it is necessary for some individuals to have certain food. Such species are adapted to this form of behaviour in so strict a manner that interference with their gregarious instincts may

Adélie Penguins returning in single file from an excursion to open water where they have been fishing. During incubation the birds of each pair take it in turn to feed, sometimes travelling a distance of 50 miles each way over the pack-ice.

Flock of Cattle Egrets on a tree serving
as sleeping-quarters.

The social relations of Galliformes vary
greatly among species. In some cases the
individuals meet only for pairing, in others,
for example Grouse (above), pairs live in
isolation, while in yet others the gregarious instinct is more or less permanent
(Vulturine Guinea-fowl, opposite).

Though colonies of Blue-footed Boobies may comprise large numbers, the nests are always well spaced out.

Adélie Penguin rookery.

result in important consequences. A case in point is the Passenger Pigeon, perhaps the most gregarious of all birds, which lived in immense flocks, estimated to be of many hundred millions—some say many thousand millions. In spite of the senseless slaughter of these birds and the rapid destruction of forests, the complete disappearance of this species in the course of a few decades can perhaps be attributed to the disturbance of its breeding behaviour. As soon as the Pigeons became rather scarce, it is probable that the necessary stimulus for breeding was lacking, their fecundity diminished considerably, and perhaps completely failed. The last specimen of the species died in captivity in 1914, but already by the end of the 19th century the bird had become very rare.

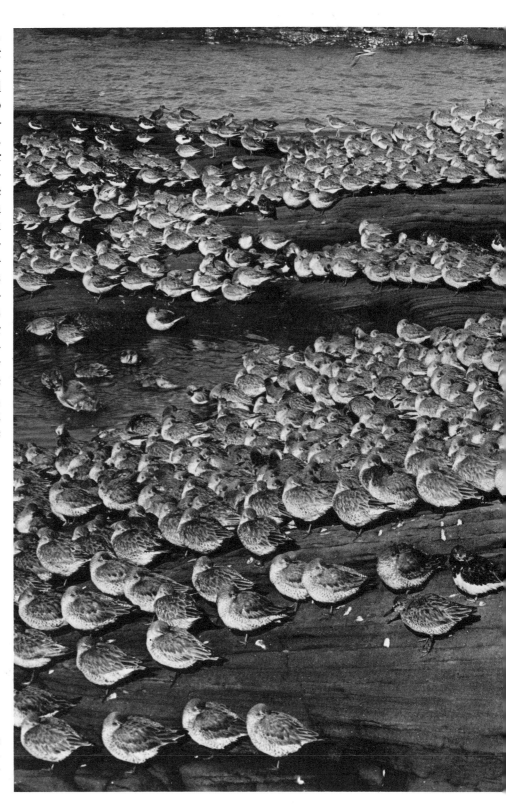

Sanderlings and a few Turnstones, a compact group of migrants which, individually, do not tolerate one another during the nesting season.

Chapter V
BIRD POPULATIONS

Natural habitats and their inhabitants

The most casual observer will soon realise that in a limited area with the same climate throughout, birds are not distributed at random. No one would think of looking for a Gull in a forest or for a Woodpecker on a beach. In choice of habitat each species has its own preference, sometimes very marked, and although some birds are gregarious, there are many which are seldom seen in company with other birds. It seems therefore of interest to enquire into the influence of various environmental factors on the distribution of birds, both with regard to locality and season.

The primary need of every animal is sufficient food. In spite of marked specific preferences, birds in general show a feeding adaptability which enables them — within certain limits — to accommodate themselves to a wide range of environments. It seems that it is the number of individuals rather than the species which is governed by food supply.

Some birds, however, have such definite food preferences that their distribution closely follows that of other animals or plants. Crossbills, which normally eat the seeds of conifers almost exclusively, live in dense growths of these trees. Although Crossbills are most numerous in northern forests of Europe, they are so attached to conifers that in the northern hemisphere they are found wherever these trees grow, even as far as the Philippines and Guatemala. The Everglade Kite is found only in the fresh-water marshes of the hot regions of America where a certain mollusc lives on which it feeds exclusively.

Everglade Kite flying over a marsh in Florida.

◀ *Pair of Mallard.*

In Africa, the distribution of the Grey Parrot coincides almost exactly with that of the oil-palm whose seeds form the bird's food.

Plants may also play a part in bird life apart from the question of food, or from such a highly developed adaptation as that of the Woodpeckers. Methods of nesting, for example, may have such exacting requirements that a species which is able to live without difficulty in a variety of environments will be restricted, at all events during the breeding season, to some particular habitat affording suitable nesting-sites. Hence the number of Tits, Starlings, or Hoopoes may depend on the occurrence of more or less decayed trees in which these birds find holes for their nests. The Great Reed-Warbler, which feeds on insects occurring anywhere in the vicinity of water, only haunts thick beds of tall reeds whose stems are partly under water, where it builds its nest. The Chaffinch lives almost anywhere so long as there are trees, even if very widely separated, in which it can nest. In addition, factors other than plants may be of significance; the Kingfisher, for example, only haunts rivers or streams with vertical banks of friable soil in which it can excavate its nest-hole.

Climatic factors are no less important than those affecting food. Each species is adapted to a life within certain limits of temperature and humidity; birds, at any rate, can withstand extremes of cold better than excessive heat, especially if the cold does not last too long. Their intense metabolism enables them to endure great cold if enough food is available, and also if they have already built up a reserve of fat; but the days must be long enough to allow time for them to collect sufficient food to produce the necessary energy. This is why in high latitudes the long winter nights, as much as temperature, influence migration. When the ground is covered with snow the feeding of many birds is impeded, and this is another factor influencing migration.

The presence of other animals may play an important part in the distribution of certain species of birds. The European Cuckoo, despite a somewhat specialised insectivorous diet, adopts the habitat of the species which it uses as fosterers for its young. Though very abundant in wooded country where both prey is plentiful and victims numerous, it is also found in high mountains well above the forest limit, where it makes use of the Black Redstart as a fosterer, and among the rocks on the sea-shore where it lays its eggs in the nests of Rock-Pipits.

In tropical savannas, herds of ruminants attract various species of birds, including the Buff-backed Heron, which feed on the insects disturbed by these great mammals. In the same way, in the Arctic, gallinaceous birds take advantage of the holes made in the snow by other animals to search for food.

It has been shown that some birds are dependent on ants or termites for their nests. The influence of man himself who, deliberately or not, may cause the dispersal of some species, must also be taken into account. It is well known what a great part he has played, unhappily, in the extinction of some birds, chiefly through the damage to—or even the destruction of—environments favourable to them.

The examination of the various factors which normally seem to govern the distribution of species often fails to explain what causes determine choice of habitat by some birds, or at least, what material advantages these afford, and some preferences have been noted which seem to be of a psychological nature.

Thus, for example, the Tree-Pipit only settles down to nest in places where there are high perches from which it descends, singing as it flies, whereas the Meadow-Pipit, which lives and nests in the same way, sings equally well when rising from the ground. Though the first species generally chooses drier ground than its near relative, the presence of perches is the main factor in its choice, since the construction of a telegraph line is enough to induce it to colonise

The Green Woodpecker, which feeds a great deal on ants which it picks up on the ground with its tongue, inhabits open country more than any other Woodpecker, but only if it is within easy reach of trees tall enough to nest in. ▶

184

damp, treeless meadows. In mountains it often reaches the upper limit of the tree line and joins, but does not penetrate, the habitat of the Water-Pipit which avoids trees, and in order to sing, takes off from a stone or rock.

Many other cases of this kind could be mentioned, for example the four species of Leaf-Warblers which nest in temperate Europe. Many, if not all, of these species may inhabit the same zone, apparently attached to certain types of undergrowth, probably as a result of rivalry among themselves.

Thus, Bonelli's Warbler, in flat country, shows a more or less exclusive preference for conifers; but it is hardly likely that the insects peculiar to such trees are indispensable, since it may be found near isolated pines in deciduous forests, but does not confine its search for food to these conifers.

In mountains this Warbler prefers to live on dry, sunny slopes covered with bushes and is an example of the variability of some birds whose habitat may change considerably from one region to

Nectar-eating birds:
a) *White-throated Honey-eater* (Melithreptus albogularis), *New Guinea;* b) *Tahiti Blue Lory* (Vini peruviana), *Society Islands;* c) *Mrs Gould's Sunbird* (Aethopyga gouldiae), *tropical Asia;* d) *Orange-breasted Flowerpecker* (Dicaeum trigonostigma), *Indo-China, Malaysia;* e) *Slender Shear-tail Humming Bird* (Doricha enicura), *Guatemala;* f) *Yellow-winged Sugar-bird or Blue Honeycreeper* (Cyanerpes cyaneus), *tropical America.*

another. The Citril Finch, the characteristic Finch of the upper limit of the forest zone in the Alps, haunts scrub right down to the shore in Corsica. The Raven occurs from the icy regions of Greenland and Spitzbergen to the northern Sahara; and the Shore-Lark [Horned Lark], which in Europe and Asia is a bird of the cold northern steppes, yet is represented in desert regions, from Rio de Oro to Mongolia. In America it is found from the coastal stretches of the Arctic Ocean to the mountains of Colombia, almost below the Equator.

The diverse habitats frequented by birds have very many intermediate stages, and the points which characterise them are so variable and numerous that no precise classification can be laid down. It is possible, however, without being too arbitrary, to establish in a very general way a few large classes with fairly constant features.

The forest environment which is found in all climates from the arctic tundra to South America and New Zealand, varies so greatly that different types of forest should be examined separately. The forests of temperate zones have been carefully studied both in Europe and in North America. There is quite a distinct difference between the inhabitants of deciduous and coniferous forests. Some birds are attached to conifers in a way which varies according to the species; thus, the Crested Tit is

only occasionally found in deciduous trees, whereas the Coal-Tit, which is quite as common in pine forests, is nevertheless found almost everywhere in small numbers.

In both these types of forest it is density of vegetation rather than its nature which influences the species of birds to be found there, and from this point of view it is interesting to trace how the fauna changes with the age of the trees. In England, in a new plantation of fir trees, the birds of the original heath area persisted for the first four years, after which they diminished in numbers, the Skylark and the Meadow-Pipit finally disappearing after nine years. The Willow-Warbler made its appearance in the fourth year, and its numbers increased until the twelfth year, when they began to diminish. The Chaffinch, Coal-Tit, and Goldcrest arrived at the end of seven years; the Tree-creeper, other Tits, and the Woodpeckers did not appear till the branches were more fully developed and it was possible to find cavities in them to nest in.

In the forests of temperate countries where the trees do not attain any great height there are hardly any birds which live consistently at any determined level. The great humid tropical forests, on the contrary, are divided into well-defined horizontal strata, each with its own fauna. On the ground, in perpetual semi-darkness and high humidity, live short-winged species which do not fly much and are often

Birds of the undergrowth of tropical forests:

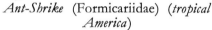

Ant-Shrike (Formicariidae) (*tropical America*)

Tit Babbler (Timaliidae) (*Malaya*)

endowed with powerful voices: Ant-Shrikes, Tinamous, Manakins in America, and Pheasants, certain Bulbuls and Babblers in tropical Asia and Malaya. Usually they are dull-coloured, which makes them difficult to see, but the brightly coloured Pittas or Jewel-Thrushes of the Old World are a notable exception. The intermediate areas, which are more or less clearly divided according to the region, constitute the habitat of Woodpeckers, Toucans, Hornbills, etc.

The tops of the trees are like another world; only here do the forest birds live in full daylight in the same way as birds of other regions which live near the ground. Here are large numbers of Parrots and many other brightly coloured birds such as Tanagers, Cotingas, Humming Birds, etc., in America, and Flycatchers, Sunbirds and many others in the Old World. The large birds of prey, ill-suited to the undergrowth, hunt in the open air.

The secondary forest which springs up after man has destroyed the primeval forest, has a special fauna somewhat resembling that found on the edges of woodland, or in gaps made by watercourses.

Between the large forest and the grassy plains all possible stages are found in different

Dupont's Lark:—Saharan Lark which matches the colour of its surroundings.

Black Wheatear.

Tits are common wherever they can find holes in which to spend the night or build their nests, whether in a tree, as in the case of this Blue Tit, or in an old wall.

The Ostrich is found in a wide variety of open habitats, such as semi-desert and grassy plains, where various animals—antelope, wildebeest, etc.—live in close proximity. They take advantage of its tallness and keen vision, which provide an early warning system when danger threatens.

Green Heron in a Florida swamp. As with the other small herons in this genus, the Green Heron is common in all tropical or semi-tropical regions.

The Red-legged Partridge, which has a restricted natural distribution (Spain and the south-west of France), is closely related to the Rock Partridge, which, however, unlike the Red-legged Partridge, with which it does not associate, inhabits mountainous regions.

Female Pin-tailed Sand-Grouse. Sand-Grouse are restricted to the arid regions of the Old World. They fly to water at a fixed time each day, sometimes covering a distance of up to 50 miles from the nest. For this purpose they gather in flocks first and are joined by others as they go.

Bonelli's Eagle. An inhabitant of dry regions of the Old World, this eagle, within the Mediterranean region, prefers low calcareous mountains with vertical rock faces for nesting.

climates, ranging from dry forest to scrubland and wooded savanna. Steppes and savannas constitute a specialised environment which affords quite different conditions of existence according to the season, and is yet further changed periodically in certain regions by the practice of "bush fires". Some seed-eating birds find an abundance of food in these localities, and many large insectivorous birds search for grasshoppers and locusts in them. The fires which adversely affect the seed-eaters are, however, favourable for insectivorous species which assemble to catch the insects driven out by the fire. Some large long-legged birds are quite characteristic of these grassy expanses. Bustards in Asia and Africa, the Secretary Bird and Ground Hornbills in Africa, Rheas on the South American pampas.

Nesting conditions in such regions are of special importance. Often large numbers of nests are built together in isolated trees; some birds such as the Burrowing Owl of the North American prairies nest in burrows. In Africa certain Larks and Chats, which require open ground, breed after the bush fires.

From the point of view of bird

191

Burrowing Owl, a small bird with long legs, is a prairie species which occurs extensively in North and South America. It nests in a burrow, preferably occupying one which has already been dug out by another animal.

Pin-tailed Sand-Grouse chick. This species inhabits semi-desert zones in the Mediterranean region and the Middle East.

White-rumped Black Wheatear.

Crowned Plover (opposite) and Senegal Bustard (below), two long-legged birds of the grassy plains of Africa.

population the cultivated countryside of our temperate regions can well be compared with the wooded savanna. Changes brought about by man have caused considerable modifications in the distribution of species. The clearing of land, especially for cereal crops, has encouraged the spread of birds of the Old World steppes such as the Skylark and Corn-Bunting. The creation of gardens and market-gardening have increased the numbers of small insectivorous birds, but against this, the larger species have almost disappeared. The draining of marshes and the construction of embankments along the rivers have resulted in a great reduction in the numbers of aquatic birds. It is in areas consisting of parks and gardens that the greatest density of birds has been noted—as many as 300 individuals to the hectare (= $2\frac{1}{2}$ acres). For comparison, the numbers of individuals per hectare found in various regions, arranged in order of numerical importance, are as follows:— 3 to 50 in the forests of Europe; 1 to 30 in the South African veldt, depending on the type of vegetation; and less than 1 during

summer in the tundras of the Arctic.

With increasing drought grassy steppes may become deserts. No species can live in absolute desert with no trace of vegetation, but a very slight amount of moisture will make it possible for a relatively abundant fauna to subsist, chiefly in stony regions. Insectivorous birds, which hardly drink at all, are found almost everywhere; seed-eaters generally require more water, and some species like the Sand-Grouse and the Desert Trumpeter Bullfinch of the deserts

of the Old World daily travel considerable distances to drink, while others, such as the Budgerigar of Australia, can do without water for quite a long time.

Adaptations to life in desert regions are found in quite varied groups. In Africa, the Courser belongs to the Limicolae; the Roadrunner of California, a Cuckoo which feeds on reptiles, has a remarkable turn of speed, and when pursued prefers to escape by running rather than by flight.

Many birds of the desert are of a uniform colour, and the colour of their plumage is adapted to that

of their surroundings. Though the similarity is often very great and the variations of some species closely follow those of the coloration of the ground, the utility of this camouflage is open to question. In any case it must be emphasised that the same adaptation is found in animals which like the Desert Eagle-Owl lead a nocturnal life and do not fear predators, and even in burrowing mammals which live underground. On the other hand, some birds have very dark plumage, such as the Black Wheatear and the Raven; it may be that carnivores avoid these conspicuous species on account of the unpleasant taste of their flesh.

As with increasing aridity the forest is replaced by desert, similarly in high latitudes the arctic tundra is reached by way of the dwarf forest. During the short summer with its long days the surface soil thaws out and many birds arrive to breed there, especially in coastal districts. It is in such regions that a large number of species of shore-birds, Geese, Ducks, etc., which visit the coasts of Europe on migration make their nests. Some Passerines, such as the Lapland Bunting and the Snow Bunting, the most northerly of all the Passerines, are peculiar to this environment. There are few birds of prey, but these are replaced by Skuas, predacious birds allied to the Gulls. In winter the Ptarmigan alone remains, often buried in the snow.

High mountains show some analogy with arctic regions, but the rarefaction of the air with the increase of altitude results in a relative dryness and creates somewhat different conditions. Some birds, for example the Snow-Finch, are peculiar to this environment and others, such as Accentors, etc., are at least almost restricted to it. A large number of characteristic northern species are found in the mountains of the northern hemisphere and are considered to be relics of the Ice Age, as for example Tengmalm's Owl, Ptarmigan, Three-toed Woodpecker, etc. Great heights may be reached, for example in the Alps where several species (Black Redstart, Wall-creeper, etc.) nest in rocks above 10,000 feet; in the Himalayas some birds occur higher than 16,000 feet and in the Great Cordillera of the Andes several species of Humming Birds obtain their sustenance from flowers near the snow-line, and nest as much as 15,000 feet or more above sea-level.

Greater Roadrunner, a Ground Cuckoo of the American south-west.

Grey Parrot. Its liking for palm-nut seeds determines its distribution and contributes to the spread of this tree in the African forests.

Cory's Shearwater on a stretch of coast in Corsica. In common with all other shearwaters, it is essentially a sea-bird, alighting on land only to nest on rocky coasts, often at a great height.

Great Black-backed Gull on nest. This large North Atlantic species has been extending its distribution southwards since the beginning of this century. Along the American coastline this increase has been to the detriment of the Herring Gull, a weaker species.

Birds of the mountains:
a) *Wall-creeper, winter plumage;* b)
Alpine Accentor; c) *Rock-Thrush;* d)
Snow-Finch; e) *Redpoll.*

Though in terrestrial environments it is almost always possible to find transitions from one type to another, the sea is a single well-defined unit, in which, nevertheless, zones with different characteristics must be distinguished.

Birds of the shore, such as Gulls, Cormorants, etc., rarely go far from the shore, and sometimes even nest near fresh water. The Alcidae, such as Guillemots, Razorbills, and Puffins, and also the Gannets, breed on shore, but for the rest of the year live at sea in the so-called neritic zone, which corresponds to the continental plateau. The high seas, the pelagic zone, are the special domain of the Procellariidae such as Shearwaters, Petrels, Albatrosses, whose distribution is correlated with that of plankton, which is specially abundant in cold waters. As a result of this fact, regions in high latitudes sometimes show a considerable density of birds whilst in warm waters there are practically uninhabited zones and several days may pass without the traveller

The Swallow-tailed Gull is a widely distributed sea-bird found among the Pacific coasts from Peru to Panama, but it breeds only in the Galapagos Islands.

sighting a single bird. Similarly the existence of cold currents explains the presence of Penguins on the south-west coasts of Africa (Benguela current) and on the Galapagos Islands almost at the equator (Humboldt current).

Female Black Redstart at nest. This species inhabits high rocky areas, commonly breeding at 6,000 ft., and as much as 16,000 ft. in the Himalayas. It is, however, widely distributed at very much lower altitudes throughout western Europe, where it breeds in town gardens and around farm buildings.

Fluctuations of populations

The quantitative study of wild animal populations, and birds in particular, is a recent science which in practice presents many difficulties. It is easy to understand how hard it is to make censuses of animals in the wild with any degree of accuracy; even simpler investigations, such as counting the number of eggs in nests, must be carried out on a very large scale if they are to serve any useful purpose. Many of the results must still be considered as provisional, but the great interest, both theoretical and practical, in everything concerning the equilibrium of nature, amply justifies the efforts of specialists, especially at a time when this equilibrium is being compromised more and more by human agency.

In spite of the difficulties inherent in such studies, results have been obtained in good enough conditions for the total population of Finches or that of Blackbirds in England to be evaluated at about 10 million. The widespread distribution of such species makes it impossible to estimate their world population with any degree of accuracy. It may be supposed, however, that it runs into hundreds of millions.

Relatively few species, of course, occur in such vast numbers, and there are inevitably considerable differences between these huge populations and those of highly localised species, often in the process of becoming extinct, which total only a few dozen individuals. The Seychelles Magpie-Robin is managing to survive—but for how long?—with twelve individuals.

In order for a population to remain stable it is evident that births must counterbalance deaths; therefore variations in fecundity and death rates are the factors which should be studied primarily.

Even under normal conditions the fecundity of any given species is variable. The average number of eggs per clutch seems to correspond to the possibilities of the parents to obtain food for the young; the number accordingly increases with the latitude, being correlated with longer days which allow the adult birds greater activity. The Robin, for example, averages 3·5 eggs per clutch in the Canary Isles as against 6·3 in Scandinavia.

In any one place at any given time, the number of eggs in a clutch seems to be independent of the density of breeding birds, that is to say, the number in any definite area, though there is a slight decrease where the density is great. Taking into account destruction by bad weather, predators, etc., about 60% of the eggs laid by small Passerines with cup-shaped nests are hatched out, and in sheltered nests the average may be higher.

There is no fixed correlation between the numbers of eggs laid and the mortality of young birds. It seems that, in certain cases at least, there is a higher death-rate in birds from large broods, especially just after the young have left the nest; the death-rate is also higher among birds of a second brood which, when they begin to be independent, encounter the rivalry of first-brood birds, which have gained in experience.

Evaluating the general rate of mortality is very difficult. It is rarely possible to determine the cause of death in birds by direct observation, and statistics obtained by various methods are sometimes open to question. The recapture of a bird ringed in the nest gives its exact age, but as the proportion of birds recovered in this way seldom exceeds 1%–2%

Bearded Vulture (Lammergeier) (Ordesa National Park in the Pyrenees). This species has been exterminated in the Swiss Alps and the Carpathians, but it survives in mountainous regions from the Mediterranean to Mongolia and China, with a few isolated populations in certain mountains of eastern and southern Africa.

the averages deduced may not be very accurate. The proportion of recoveries is greater among game-birds, but this particular cause of mortality does not permit generalisations. Other inapparent factors difficult to detect may falsify the results, as, for example, loss of rings among sea-birds on account of corrosion.

Attempts can also be made to ascertain by direct observation the survival of individual birds identifiable by means of coloured rings worn on the feet. But this would require their being constant to one particular locality, which cannot be proved a priori.

Nevertheless, the figures obtained make it possible to form a fairly accurate idea of the composition of bird populations according to age. The annual mortality rate among the small Passerines is high. In the case of an African Waxbill (Estrilda) it has been assessed as high as 75%, but for the most part it is around 50%—that is to say, in every 100 individuals about 50 are one year old, 25 two years old, 12 three years old, and so on. This 50% mortality rate is also found among Ducks and gallinaceous birds; it falls to 30%–40% among the Limicolae and Gulls. The lowest rate seems to be that of a colony of Albatrosses, estimated at 3%.

Quite often mortality is very high in young birds; it has been estimated that in a certain population of Terns, where more than 110,000 birds were ringed, there was a mortality of 95% during the first winter. Populations of

breeding birds therefore contain a large majority of old birds; for example, in a flock of Oyster-catchers the average age was 13 and some birds were even 23 years old.

These results show that birds which die of old age are in a very small minority, as their potential longevity is much greater. Despite their intense metabolism, small Passerines may live more than twenty years in captivity, which is a much greater age than that attained by mammals of the same size. Geese may live more than thirty years, Cranes and Eagles forty years, Ravens, Condors, Pelicans and Parrots sixty or more. The age limit does not depend entirely on size and Ostriches rarely live to be forty.

Three main factors affecting mortality can be distinguished: lack of food, diseases, and predatism.

The consequences of the decrease in food resources vary according to whether the birds are non-migrant species or ones which tend to move on quickly from one place to another. Similarly, birds with a varied diet are more resistant than those which have a highly specialised diet.

Bird diseases have been studied in depth, but the way in which they arise and their influence on bird populations remain, on the whole, matters of conjecture.

It is noteworthy that the effects of these various factors are far from always being independent of one another. When food is scarce, weakened individuals are

more susceptible to diseases and more likely to fall victims to predators than in normal conditions. The latter, for their part, by eliminating individuals already affected, can halt the onset of an epidemic, thus rendering a useful service to the populations of their prey.

In speaking of stable populations, the definition of this term must be properly understood; there is never an entirely stable population, even if seasonal fluctuations resulting from births are taken into account. In normal conditions the variations from one year to another are always slight, but exceptional circumstances, such as an unusually hard winter, produce considerable modifications to the populations. The important fact is that in such cases losses are rapidly made good and the original numbers restored.

At the limit of normal expansion, on the other hand, losses can only be made good with difficulty, and some birds disappear entirely for a period of years, or again, given favourable conditions, may for a time be found in numbers beyond the usual limit. Examples of the latter are the fluctuations of Cetti's Warbler and the Fantail Warbler in France.

The question arises therefore: how is this stable population assured, and by what process do

Birds of the Mediterranean region:
a) *Roller;* b) *Bee-eater;* c) *Dartford Warbler;* d) *Pratincole;* e) *Black-eared Wheatear (black-throated form).* ▶

Both Hornbills and Touracos, represented here by the African Grey Hornbill (left) and the Blue-crested Touraco (below), feed mainly on fruit. Both are found not only in tropical forests but also in dry wooded savannas.

The Bald Ibis, which, unlike most other ibises, avoids damp regions, was found in Europe as late as the seventeenth century, but is now confined to certain localities in North Africa and the Middle East.

Snowy Owl. The periodic fluctuations in population of this species have been closely studied.

births and deaths counterbalance one another exactly? This vitally important question, which connotes that of the "balance of nature" itself, is the same for all living creatures and is extremely difficult to resolve on account of the immense complexity of the factors involved. It may be said that anything which occurs in the life of the individual forms part of the data of this general problem.

So far as birds are concerned, it may be supposed that the mechanism of natural selection has led them to rear the largest possible number of young and that, on the other hand, their losses become proportionately greater as the population density increases. As the death-rate rises with the density the balance is automatically kept constant.

Food is the chief factor in this mechanism, on the one hand through its abundance during the breeding season in order to augment the population, and on the other its scarcity outside this period, which reduces the numbers. Thus, in temperate regions for example, the extended nesting period which comprises long days results for many species in large numbers of young which are easy to feed and which by the autumn, therefore, are very numerous. The rigours of winter for the non-migrant birds and the hazards of long journeys for the migrants, however, bring about a high death-rate which counterbalances the density increase.

In certain cases, however, the rate of reproduction appears to remain well below its potential. In the tropical forests many species, mainly fruit-eating ones, rear a very small number of young (an annual clutch of two eggs) in spite of the abundance of resources and the fact that only the female feeds the young. It must be admitted then that, through the agency of natural selection, the birth-rate has adapted itself to the mortality factors, thus avoiding a useless expenditure of energy.

It is impossible at the present time to give a definite answer to the question. The habits of birds, moreover, are too diverse for anyone to be able to prove *a priori* that the regulation mechanism is the same for all species, and, despite all the efforts of specialists so far, much more research is needed before this question can be satisfactorily answered.

Some variations recur with extraordinary regularity; this is most frequent in birds of the arctic regions, in which the period is 3 or 4 years in the tundras and 9 or 10 years in the forests in the extreme north of America. The best known case is that of the Snowy Owl which lives on lemmings. These small arctic rodents provide an ideal example of animals with periodic fluctuations; in some years they are very rare and, being nocturnal, are almost impossible to find; when, however, their numbers increase,

Pallas's Sand-Grouse.

they swarm to such an extent that they set out on long journeys in broad daylight, collecting in vast hordes in some places: subsequently their numbers diminish as fast as they increased and they once more disappear. Snowy Owls, which lay more eggs when their prey is plentiful, have a cycle of 3 to 4 years, which corresponds exactly to that of the lemmings; foxes also follow the same cycle.

In the forests of North America a similar phenomenon, with a period of 9 to 10 years, is found; the fluctuations of the American hare coincide with those of the Great Horned Owl and the Goshawk, as well as those of the Canadian lynx. It seems very probable that the fluctuations of the small mammals are the direct cause of those of the birds of prey and carnivores, but corresponding variations are found in other birds — the Ruffed Grouse in America, the Willow Grouse in northern Europe—which are not predatory. It is tempting to assume that climatic conditions which act simultaneously on both rodents and gallinaceous birds account for this, but in point of fact the periods of abundance of

these two groups do not coincide. Nor does it seem that infectious diseases can be responsible, as no disease is known to be common to both these groups. It may be that predators themselves, birds of prey and carnivores, form the connecting link between the cycles of rodents and gallinaceous birds as when rodents become scarce the predators feed on birds, which are not their normal food, and thus affect their numbers. Owing to insufficient data this attractive hypothesis cannot be confirmed, and as, in any case, mammalogists have been unable to determine with any certainty what causes fluctuations in rodents, nothing positive can be affirmed regarding these problems.

After the disappearance of the lemmings, the Snowy Owls disperse in search of food, and thus appear at regular intervals in places far distant from their normal habitat. There are other invasions which seem more difficult to explain, and although those of the Waxwing tend to be repeated every ten years, most of them are quite irregular. Invasions occur in many regions, those of Pallas's Sand-Grouse of the

Asiatic steppes have resulted in large numbers of these birds travelling as far as Western Europe, where even nesting has been recorded; it is, however, the irruptions from northern forests which have been most thoroughly studied, chiefly in Europe.

The species concerned in these mass exoduses, in winter at all events, only subsist on the seeds of a very few plants, principally conifers, and it seems likely that the invasions of birds such as Crossbills, Nutcrackers, Waxwings, etc., are correlated with a failure of the seed supply in their normal range. It has not been possible, however, to establish the precise reason for this phenomenon, and further it should be noted that between these very general movements and normal winter displacements, which are more or less true migrations, there are all intermediate stages. This phenomenon on a smaller scale is not rare in many species which are not regular migrants, such as the Jay, Tits and the Greater Spotted Woodpecker. What is more difficult to understand is the distance covered once the impulse is given to a large number of individuals, as in the case of the lemmings, which, arriving at the coast, continue to swim out to sea till they are drowned. These mass migrations generally end with the death of the individuals taking part in them as they do not colonise the countries invaded. In a few cases, however, a partial return to their place of origin has been noted.

The extension and reduction of the range of a species is not unusual. This is usually a slow process and can only be appreciated by keeping a very close watch, but observations made over an adequate period show that the changes may be considerable.

It has been possible to follow, often accurately, modifications caused by changes in climate in Europe at the present time. The warmer springs and summers in the north have been followed by the extension in the range of

many species; in Sweden, for example, several, such as the Jay, Greenfinch, and Blue Tit, have spread northwards, others, such as the Golden Oriole, which only appeared accidentally, now breed there; on the contrary, northern species, such as the Siberian Jay, are decreasing. Similarly in Iceland, despite its isolation, several species from further south have become established, including two land birds, the Starling and the Short-eared Owl, but in the northern part of the island the numbers of the Long-tailed Duck [Old-Squaw] and Little Auk have decreased.

Some expansions, which can be extremely rapid, do not appear to be in any way connected with climatic changes. That of the Serin began in the last century and this little bird of the Mediter-

ranean region is now found throughout the whole of Europe; it even shows signs of wintering there.

The Fieldfare, which breeds in northern Europe, spread from East Prussia south-westwards a century ago and now nests in eastern France. But the most remarkable example in our regions is provided by the Eastern Collared Turtle Dove, an Asiatic bird which before 1930 did not occur further west than the Balkans. Its rapid but sporadic spread has resulted in its being observed as far afield as Scotland and Scandinavia.

In the 18th century the most southerly breeding limit of the Fulmar, an arctic species, was just north of Iceland and St Kilda, the most westerly island of the Hebrides. About the middle of that

Spread of the Fulmar on the coasts of the British Isles. Black indicates breeding grounds and dots non-breeding birds.

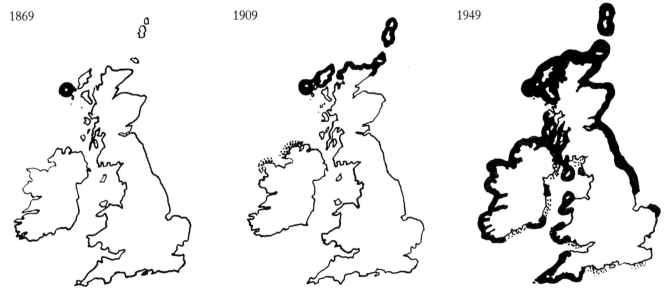

1869   1909   1949

century it colonised the entire Icelandic coastline and later nearly all the coasts of Britain, and now it nests in Brittany. Its expansion has been attributed to the resources provided by the cutting up of whales and later by the trawlers fishing in the open sea. Since, however, its population has increased only slightly in Norway and not at all along the coasts of America where prevailing conditions are similar, it is doubtful whether this explanation carries much weight.

Finally, there is the most spectacular example of all—the Cattle Egret of the hot regions of Africa and Asia, which, northwards, does not extend beyond Andalusia and southern Japan. After crossing the Atlantic it appeared as a very occasional visitor on the north-west coast of South America. In 1930 it began to settle in British Guiana and has since swarmed southwards and even more so northwards. Flourishing colonies exist in Florida, where as many as 30,000 individuals have been counted in winter flocks, and it is now spreading into Ontario and Newfoundland. Via New Guinea the Asiatic populations have reached Australia, where the species is now expanding.

Little need be said here of expansions such as those of the House-Sparrow and Starling, due to their artificial introduction into various places, or of reductions brought about by human agency, which in some cases have led to total extinction. The main causes have been the destruction of natural habitats, the introduction of domestic animals or vermin such as rats, intensive hunting and, nowadays, the ever-growing pollution of a variety of environments contaminated by industrial waste and the use of pesticides.

Certain regressions are due to entirely natural causes such as climatic changes, referred to above. Others are somewhat enigmatic. It is perhaps merely a question of the decline of species which were in process of disappearing, just as many others have disappeared ever since life began on earth.

Fulmar.

The Horned Parrakeet of New Caledonia, one example among many of island species threatened with extinction through modifications made by man to their natural environment.

In America the Scrub Jay has a discontinuous distribution. A distance of almost 900 miles separates Florida from the western regions, where it occurs from the State of Washington southwards as far as Mexico.

Collared Dove. The spectacular spread of this species has been facilitated by its ability to adapt to human environments.

CONCLUSION

In conclusion it would be interesting to attempt to explain the various aspects of bird psychology, so far as it can be understood at present. Unfortunately, so complicated and difficult a subject cannot be dealt with in a few pages, even briefly. Birds are first-class material for the study of psychological phenomena. Mammals, being closer to us in body structure, might seem to be more easily understood, but many lead a nocturnal life, and their actions are largely controlled by a world of scents into which we cannot enter. Birds live before us in a world of sight and sound, apparently not very different from our own, and where, at all events, investigations are much easier. Indeed bird watching is responsible for an important part of the progress that has been made in the study of animal psychology.

For a long time, interpretations of the actions of animals, even those made by the most experienced naturalists, were based on human sentiments. It has been common to speak of duty, jealousy and hatred, and to admire the pity and compassion of a bird feeding young ones other than its own. Instinct was certainly taken into consideration, but so vaguely that the term itself ceased to have any exact significance.

The reaction against these oversimplified sentimental interpretations has resulted in a tendency to see, in manifestations of animal life, only automatic, innate responses to internal or external "stimuli", and in a way to study these facts in the same spirit as physico-chemical phenomena in a laboratory. Whilst not denying the interest of this aspect in so far as the control of any study is concerned, it seems necessary to guard against too rigid an outlook.

To compare an animal with a machine is almost as anthropomorphic as comparing it to man; in this case man could not conceive that anything but himself and the objects he can create, or their equivalents, could exist. The higher animals have obviously points in common with both man and machines, but they are actually neither one nor the other, and therefore often very difficult to understand.

The preceding chapters have shown to what extent birds are creatures of instinct, whose "knowledge" is for the most part inborn, and whose actions depend on physiological conditions as much as on external circumstances. Observations, however, provide strong evidence that birds must experience emotions. Though it may not be going too far to speak of fear or hunger, for instance, it is clear that the emotions of an animal are impossible to define. We know our own by introspection, and can deduce those of our fellows by analogy, but we have no basis for those of birds. All one can say is that they must be little differentiated, judging especially by the ease with which apparently similar manifestations occur in different circumstances; this uniformity also gives a reasonable explanation of the frequent occurrence of "substitutional activities".

Though instinctive actions control a bird's life, it manifests many others which cannot be defined as "intelligence", in default of a good definition of the

Birds of the temperate Eurasian forest:
a), b) *Male and female Siskin;* c), d) *Female and male Bullfinch;* e) *Firecrest;* f) *Goldcrest;* g) *Black Woodpecker.*

209

term, but which denote highly developed adaptation to circumstances, learning by experience, powers of observation, and memory. Some actions which it is tempting to call premeditated are undoubtedly innate, as, for example, those of the Woodpecker-finch of the Galapagos Islands using a thorn to poke into holes in bark to dislodge insects which its beak cannot reach. On the other hand, activities such as the recognition of individuals, which is developed to a degree of perfection which we ourselves can attain only with our fellow men, must result from the personal experience of the subject, even though it is based on a particular innate aptitude.

As an example of how far it is possible for spontaneous adaptation to new circumstances to go, may be mentioned the case of Tits, which, chiefly in England, have acquired the habit of opening milk bottles. In some districts milk in bottles, with a metal or paper top, is left on the doorsteps in the morning. Tits and some other species have learned to pierce and remove these tops in order to drink the milk. The remarkable thing is that this habit has originated independently in various widely separated localities, and each time has spread rapidly by a kind of "emulation" which is quite obscure.

Experiments have shown that some birds possess very specialised attributes. Ravens, for example, were able to recognise a number of objects—up to 6—set before them, either simultaneously, or one after the other, and irrespective of the nature of the objects or the manner of their arrangement. For this, an exacting training was necessary, and the subjects were obviously under extremely artificial conditions. The fact is not so interesting in itself, but it demonstrates the existence of potential faculties, and it cannot be affirmed *a priori* that under normal conditions these are never manifested, though in a rudimentary fashion. It is also well to remember that the very diverse individual attitudes shown by birds when trained should be a warning against too mechanistic an explanation of their actions.

It is particularly difficult to judge knowledge acquired by birds, as it often seems to disappear before purely instinctive manifestations, and actions occur which superficially may seem stupid. There is the classic case of Jackdaws at liberty which became so tame as to allow their

210

nests to be examined without any reaction, they knew each other individually and also easily recognised people familiar to them, but they attacked their guardian one day when he had a wet pair of black bathing-drawers in his hand. A study of their reactions showed that defence of a comrade in danger is automatically released in this species by the sight of a black, shining object in an unusual place for a Jackdaw. In such a case none of the individually acquired knowledge seems to persist and this reaction to isolated factors — "stimuli" to use the specialists' term—rather than to the situation as a whole, is characteristic of instinctive actions. In the preceding chapters, other examples, such as the feeding of the young Cuckoo, have been given.

Whatever difficulties the study of animal psychology may present, it ought to be one of the chief concerns of zoologists. Apart from the subject itself, it must be admitted that, though the human mind may have powers which are not found in animals, there are certainly points in common. Just as the study of comparative anatomy and physiology of the higher vertebrates has assisted considerably in obtaining knowledge of the structure of the human frame, so should the study of animal psychology help to a better understanding of a number of human actions. Very often acquired habits may obscure the basic instinct, but, to quote only simple actions, should it not be admitted that the gesture of a person scratching his head when unable to make up his mind

between two opposing inclinations is very analogous to, if not identical with, "substitution activities" such as a bird beginning to preen its feathers when its nest is threatened? Similarly does not the familiar unconscious infectiousness of yawning resemble certain collective stimulations?

It would be easy to find other analogies, and for actions of much greater consequence both for the individual and for the society. It is not by investing animals with human feeling that we shall feel they are nearer to us, or that we shall understand them better, but, on the contrary, by recognising that it is man who, without realising it and despite his isolation, has retained many psychological characteristics of the higher animals.

Whinchat attacking a stuffed Cuckoo.

Cattle Egrets. Here the young, already fully developed but not yet having left the colony, climb up the branches to meet the parent bird.

CLASSIFICATION OF BIRDS

STRUTHIONIFORMES: Struthionidae (*Ostriches*); Rheidae (*Rheas*); Casuariidae (*Cassowaries, Emu*).

APTERYGIFORMES: Apterygidae (*Apteryx or Kiwis*).

SPHENISCIFORMES: Spheniscidae (*Penguins*).

PODICIPIFORMES: Podicipidae (*Grebes*); Gaviidae (*Divers* [*Loons*]).

ALCIFORMES: Alcidae (*Auks, Guillemots, Puffins, etc.*), a group sometimes closely related to the Laridae.

PROCELLARIIFORMES: Diomedeidae (*Albatrosses*); Procellariidae (*Petrels, Shearwaters*); Hydrobatidae (*Storm Petrels*); etc.

PELECANIFORMES: Phalacrocoracidae (*Cormorants*); Sulidae (*Gannets*); Pelecanidae (*Pelicans*); etc.

CICONIIFORMES: Plataleidae (*Spoonbills, Ibises*); Ardeidae (*Herons, Bitterns, Night Herons, etc.*); Scopidae (*Hammerheaded Stork*); Ciconiidae (*Storks*); etc.

ANSERIFORMES: Phoenicopteridae (*Flamingos*); Anseridae or Anatidae (*Geese, Swans, Ducks, Sawbills, etc.*).

LARIFORMES: Laridae (*Gulls, Terns or Sea Swallows, Scissorbills*); Stercorariidae (*Skuas*).

CHARADRIIFORMES: Chionidae (*Sheathbills*); Glareolidae (*Pratincoles, Coursers*); Charadriidae or Limicolae (*Woodcock, Godwits, Curlews, Sandpipers, Plovers, Phalaropes, etc.*); Jacanidae (*Jacanas*); etc.

RALLIFORMES OR GRUIFORMES: Burhinidae (*Stone Curlew*); Otidae (*Bustards*); Gruidae (*Cranes*); Rallidae (*Rails, Moorhens, Coots*); Turnicidae (*Hemipodes*); etc.

TINAMIFORMES: Tinamidae (*Tinamous*).

GALLIFORMES: Tetraonidae (*Capercaillie, Grouse*); Phasianidae (*Pheasants, Partridges, Guinea-fowl, etc.*); Cracidae (*Curassows*); Megapodiidae (*Megapodes*); etc.

COLUMBIFORMES: Pterocletidae (*Pin-tailed Sand-Grouse, Sand-Grouse*); Columbidae (*Pigeons*); Raphidae (*Dodo*).

FALCONIFORMES: Vulturidae (*American Vultures, Condors, American Black Vulture*); Sagittariidae (*Secretary Birds*); Falconidae (*Vultures of the Old World, Goshawks, Sparrow-Hawks, Buzzards, Eagles, Kites, Falcons, etc.*).

STRIGIFORMES: Strigidae (*Owls*). *This order is sometimes closely related to the* Coraciadiformes *or the* Caprimulgiformes.

PSITTACIFORMES: Psittacidae (*Parrots*).

CUCULIFORMES: Cuculidae (*Cuckoos, Anis, etc.*); Musophagidae (*Touracos*).

PICIFORMES: Picidae (*Woodpeckers, Wrynecks*); Indicatoridae (*Honeyguides*); Capitonidae (*Barbets*); Rhamphastidae (*Toucans*); Bucconidae (*Puffbirds*); etc.

TROGONIFORMES: Trogonidae (*Trogons*).

CAPRIMULGIFORMES: Caprimulgidae (*Goatsuckers or Nightjars*); Podargidae (*Frogmouths*); Steatornithidae (*Oil-Birds*).

APODIFORMES: Apodidae (*Swifts*); Trochilidae (*Humming Birds*).

COLIIFORMES: Coliidae (*Colies or Mouse-birds*).

CORACIADIFORMES: Coraciidae (*Rollers*); Meropidae (*Bee-eaters*); Alcedinidae (*Kingfishers*); Bucerotidae (*Hornbills*); Upupidae (*Hoopoes*).

PASSERIFORMES: *This order, which includes more than half the known species of birds, is not, from the point of view of classification, more important than the others. It is extremely complex, the divisions that can be established are even less well defined, the distinctions used are slight, and the beak, to which the earlier authors attached great importance, can only be considered a secondary characteristic. Actually it varies considerably in certain natural groups, and in one species even differs in the male and the female. Owing to the great number of divisions it is only possible to mention some of the more important groups.*

Series of the Tracheophonae: *Ant-Thrushes, Ant-Shrikes, Woodhewers, Oven-Birds.*

Series of the Oligomyodae: *Tyrants, Manakins, Cotingas, Pittas.*

Series of the Acromyodae: *The division into families is very complex and their order more or less arbitrary. The principal ones are:*

Menuridae (*Lyre-Birds*).

Muscicapidae (*Flycatchers, Warblers, Thrushes, Chats, Nightingales, etc.*).

Troglodytidae (*Wrens*).

Dicruridae (*Drongos*).

Laniidae (*Shrikes*).

Paridae (*Tits*).

Hirundinidae (*Swallows*).

Nectariniidae (*Sunbirds*).

Meliphagidae (*Honey-eaters*).

Fringillidae (*Chaffinches, Bullfinches, Goldfinches, Crossbills, Buntings, etc.*).

Ploceidae (*Sparrows, Weavers, Whydahs*).

Alaudidae (*Larks*).

Motacillidae (*Wagtails, Pipits*).

Icteridae (*Caciques, Cowbirds, Troupials, etc.*).

Sturnidae (*Starlings, etc.*).

Paradisaeidae (*Birds of Paradise, Bower-Birds*).

Corvidae (*Ravens, Crows, Magpies, Jays, Nutcrackers, Siberian Jay, etc.*).

ACKNOWLEDGMENTS

The colour plates on pages 33, 36, 55, 143, 186, 196, 201 and 208 were painted by Paul Barruel.

The photographs reproduced in this work were supplied by:

Australian News and Information Service: 112.
John Barlee: 14, 69, 163, 169.
René Bille: 54 (top, centre).
Boudoint: 42.
Als Britten: 133.
Dr J. Burnier: 54 (bottom), 98 (bottom).
Dr Cendron—Expéditions polaires françaises: 93 (bottom).
Norman Chaffer: 86 (bottom).
Jean-Claude Chantelat: 9, 24 (bottom right), 32, 39 (top), 92 (bottom), 95 (top), 105, 106 (top left, bottom right), 108, 109 (top, bottom right), 115, 117 (top left, bottom), 123, 128 (top right), 129 (top), 130 (top), 131 (bottom), 137 (top, bottom left), 144, 172, 185, 189 (top), 190 (top right), 195 (bottom right).
C. Douglas Deane: 57 (left and right).
Dragesco: 113.
H. Friedmann: 173.
René Gacond: 64, 122 (top), 139, 140, 147.
Ron Garrison—San Diego Zoo Photog, 35 (top), 153.
Paul Géroudet: 26 (top), 106 (top right), 129 (bottom), 130 (right), 157 (bottom), 168 (bottom).
Werner Haller: 13, 39 (bottom), 109 (bottom left), 111, 122 (bottom).
K. A. Hindwood: 94 (top), 97 (right).
Eric Hosking: 16, 21 (bottom), 22 (top), 28 (top), 29, 44, 51 (top), 60, 66 (right and left), 67, 70, 75, 88, 94 (bottom), 96, 99 (bottom), 114, 118, 126, 132, 151, 171, 181, 210, 211.
Jacana—André Bayle: 37 (top), 125 (bottom).

Jacana—M. Brosselin: 47, 49 (top), 51 (bottom), 156, 192 (right), 194.
Jacana—H. Chaumeton: 93 (top), 150.
Jacana—Serge Chevalier: 182.
Jacana—Manfred Danegger: 22 (bottom).
Jacana—Dubois: 117 (top right), 190 (bottom).
Jacana—André Fatras: 45, 59, 90 (bottom), 127, 128 (top left), 141, 198, 206.
Jacana—J. and M. Fievet: 34 (bottom).
Jacana—Marc Lélo: 10.
Jacana—Letellier: 8.
Jacana—Mac Warren: 106 (bottom left).
Jacana—Maes: 61.
Jacana—P. Montoya: 124, 179 (left).
Jacana—Cl. Nardin: 130 (bottom).
Jacana—Pierre Petit: 50, 134.
Jacana—J. Prévost: 125 (top), 136.
Jacana—B. Rebouleau: 38 (left).
Jacana—Francis Roux: 30, 71, 148, 152, 162.
Jacana—W. Schraml: 46 (top right).
Jacana—Suinot: 180 (bottom).
Jacana—Benoit Tollu: 56 (bottom).
Jacana—Usclat: 48 (top).
Jacana—J.-Philippe Varin: 25 (bottom).
Jacana—Yves Vial: 207 (bottom).
Jacana—J. Vielliard: 46 (top left).
Jacana—Vienne: 37 (bottom), 73.
Jacana—Albert Visage: 12 (top), 199.
R. E. Johnson: 58.
Kirschner—Expéditions polaires françaises: 170, 175 (top), 176.
F. P. J. Kooymans: 77 (top and centre), 83.
Norman Laird: 19.
E. H. N. Lowther: 99 (top), 101.
E. Meier Jr: 158 (bottom), 167, 168 (top), 179 (top right, bottom).
New York Zoological Society: 79, 85.

New Zealand-American Fiorland Expedition: 100 (bottom), 107.
Nils J. Nilsson: 100 (top).
Alwin Pedersen: 43 (left), 68, 103, 124, 161.
Lord William Percy: 49 (bottom), 131 (top).
Petersen: 40.
W. W. A. Phillips: 97 (left).
Pommier—Expéditions polaires françaises: 174.
Niall Rankin: 102, 175 (bottom).
Rapho—Pasquier: 82 (top).
Rapho—Christian Zuber: 56 (top), 180 (top), 197, 202 (top), 207 (top right).
Ripley: 86 (top).
Dr Sapin-Jaloustre—Expéditions polaires françaises: 95 (bottom), 178.
Ch. W. Schwartz: 74.
Michael Sharland: 104.
Severn Wildfowl Trust: 87.
Jacques Six: 11, 24 (top).
H. Sick: 89.
Stuart Smith: 121.
Dr E. Sutter: 117, 166.
P. O. Swanberg: 31, 119, 120.
C. W. Teager: 48 (bottom).
J.-F. and M. Terrasse: 12 (bottom), 24 (left), 25 (top), 26 (bottom), 34 (top), 35 (bottom), 41, 46 (bottom), 52, 76, 91, 92 (top), 137 (bottom right), 138, 157 (top), 158 (top left), 177, 183, 189 (bottom), 190 (top left), 191, 192 (top left, bottom), 193, 195 (top, bottom left), 202 (bottom), 207 (top right).
Van Someren: 84.
Van Riper: 27.
Ch. Vaucher: 98 (top), 135.
G. K. Yeates: 90 (top), 98 (centre).

Photo Gallet, p. 38 (right): from *Les Flamants roses de Camargue* by E. Gallet, pub. Payot-Lausanne.
Photos Millon, p. 43 (right): from *Le Traité de Zoologie* by P. Grassé, pub. Masson.

BIBLIOGRAPHY

General

AUSTIN, O. Jr. and SINGER, A.: *Birds of the World* (Paul Hamlyn, 1962). Contains some of the finest of Arthur Singer's illustrations.

FISHER, J.: *Birds as Animals* (Heinemann, 1939).

FISHER, J. and PETERSON, R. T.: *The World of Birds* (MacDonald, 1964).

LANDSBOROUGH THOMSON, A. (ed.): *A New Dictionary of Birds* (Nelson, 1964). A mine of information on every aspect of bird biology.

PETERSON, R. T.: *The Birds* (Time-Life, 1963).

SMITH, S.: *How to Study Birds* (Collins, 1945).

VAN TYNE, J. and BERGER, A. J.: *Fundamentals of Ornithology* (John Wiley and Sons, New York, 1959).

WELTY, J. C.: *The Life of Birds* (Saunders, London and Philadelphia, 1962).

Birds and their environment

LACK, D.: *Natural Regulations of Animal Numbers* (Oxford University Press, 1954).

— *Population Studies of Birds* (Oxford University Press, 1966).

— *Ecological Adaptations for Breeding in Birds* (Methuen, 1968).

Physiology and behaviour

ARMSTRONG, E. A.: *Bird Display and Behaviour* (Lindsay Drummond, 1947). This book is of far wider interest than is indicated by the title.

HINDE, R.: *Bird Vocalizations* (Cambridge University Press, 1970).

LORENZ, K.: *King Solomon's Ring* (Methuen, 1952). A delightful account in popular language of the author's views.

MARSHALL, A. J.: *Biology and Comparative Physiology of Birds* (Academic Press, London and New York, 1960–61, 2 vols.).

MATTHEWS, G. V. T.: *Bird Navigation* (2nd edn., Cambridge University Press, 1968).

THORPE, W. H.: *Learning and Instinct in Animals* (Harvard University Press, 1956).

Bird Song (Cambridge University Press, 1960).

TINBERGEN, N.: *The Study of Instinct* (Oxford University —Press, 1951).

Bird identification

1 Europe

GILLIARD, E. T.: *Living Birds of the World* (Hamish Hamilton, 1958).

PETERSON, R. T., MOUNTFORT, G. and HOLLOM, P. A. D.: *A Field Guide to the Birds of Britain and Europe* (Collins, 1954).

VOOUS, K. H.: *Atlas of European Birds* (Nelson, 1960). A detailed account of the distribution and biology of European species.

WITHERBY, H. F., JOURDAIN, F. C. R., TICEHURST, N. F. and TUCKER, B. W.: *The Handbook of British Birds* (Witherby, 5 vols., 1938–41).

2 North America

GODFREY, W. E.: *The Birds of Canada* (National Museum of Canada, 1966).

PETERSON, R. T.: *A Field Guide to the Birds* (Houghton Mifflin, Boston, 1947).

ROBBINS, C. S., BRUUN, B. and ZIM, H. S.: *Birds of North America* (Golden Press, New York, 1966). Colour illustrations by Arthur Singer.

3 West Indies

BOND, J.: *Birds of the West Indies* (Collins, 1960). Colour illustrations by Don R. Eckelberry.

HAVERSCHMIDT, F.: *Birds of Surinam* (Oliver and Boyd, 1968). Colour plates by Paul Barruel. Essential for French Guiana.

Ornithological journals and periodicals

1 British

Birds (The Royal Society for the Protection of Birds).

Bird Life (Junior magazine) (The Royal Society for the Protection of Birds).

Bird Study (The British Trust for Ornithology).

Ibis (The British Ornithologists' Union).

2 North American

The *Audubon* Magazine (formerly known as *Bird Lore*) (The National Audubon Society).

The Auk (The American Ornithologists' Union).

The Condor (The Cooper Ornithological Society).

Wilson's Bulletin (The Wilson's Ornithological Club).

INDEX

Page numbers in roman refer to the text. Those in italic refer to the illustrations.

217